Treasure of Kenya

TREASURE OF
KENYA

BY
THE RT. HON.
Malcolm MacDonald

ILLUSTRATED
WITH PHOTOGRAPHS BY
Christina Loke

Collins

ST JAMES'S PLACE · LONDON

1965

To
FIONA
with love

Contents

Acknowledgements

We are deeply indebted to the following game wardens and other experts for their wise guidance on safaris in various regions of Kenya: Lyn Temple-Boreham, Bill Langridge, Larry Wateridge, Chris Megson, David Roberts, Rodney Elliott, Freddie Seed, Stephen Ellis, J. A. Dawson, the late Barry Chapell, and numerous of their African game-scouts and assistants. They are all members of a devoted team of men whose work over the years has done much to achieve the intelligent preservation of Kenya's wild life. We are grateful also to John Karmali, Wali Mohamed, Masood Quraishi and T. A. Abraham in Nairobi for aid on various technicalities connected with the photography for this book. And we express warm thanks to that distinguished trio Ian Grimwood (who was then Kenya's Chief Game Warden), Mervyn Cowie (the Director of the Kenya National Parks) and John Williams of the Coryndon Museum, who is East Africa's best ornithologist, for invaluable help in selecting our illustrations from thousands of pictures taken by the photographer, and in reading and correcting the author's manuscript.

CHRISTINA LOKE
MALCOLM MACDONALD

Photographer's Note

Mr. Malcolm MacDonald and I had already collaborated on two books, *Birds in my Indian Garden* and *Birds in the Sun*; and I honestly did not think that I could attempt this third one when Malcolm asked me to do so. He suggested that I should photograph not only the birds of Kenya, but the animals too—an expert operation which I had never tried before. It was due to Malcolm's tactful persuasion, flattery, and confidence in my photography that—armed with two Nikkorex cameras, tripods, countless films, Ascor electronic flash equipment, expedition clothes, and many other essential paraphernalia—I set out from Singapore for Nairobi and the beginning of my three months safari in Africa. I had heard tales from other travellers about the fabulous Nairobi National Park, and been told that one is often greeted on arrival in Nairobi by herds of giraffes, zebras and other wild beasts strolling near the airport; so when my plane touched down there I was relieved to be greeted instead by a beautiful apparition in the form of Audrey MacDonald herself, who had come to the airport to welcome me.

The very next day I was taken to the National Park by the game warden, and realised immediately what a different technique from that to which I was accustomed I would have to adopt to photograph the animals and birds when stalking them there. I had brought with me the ordinary 1·4 cm., 135 cm. and 200 cm. as well as the 350 cm. and 400 cm. lenses. Except when I used the 1·4 cm. and 135 cm. lenses I was never able to hold the camera steady inside a tripod-less land-rover. So I immediately ordered two very solid clamps which I attached in each side-window of a seat in the vehicle. By doing this I was able to move quickly from side to side of the land-rover and take photographs according to the light conditions and the positioning of the animals. I would like to mention that I am very grateful to Bill Langridge, who accompanied me on practically all my safaris, and became my guide and driver. He was an expert at taking me as close as possible to the animals without frightening them. Before long, Bill knew exactly what angles I wanted to shoot from; and his skill at positioning me at the right distance from my subjects, depending on the lens I was using and the direction of the sun, was amazing. It took me nearly three weeks of trial, error and disappointments to learn the right techniques. Quick reflexes and swift action were very necessary in that animal photography, otherwise I would get pictures only of the beasts' buttocks and tails disappearing behind bushes. I had also just changed my camera from a 4 × 5 Speedgraphic to a 35 mm. Nikkorex, and this was my first experience with the handling of that small camera.

The photographs of birds were taken partly at their nests from a hide, and partly by stalking them. I used my electronic flash of 1/25,000th of a second for the flight pictures of the smaller birds. The pictures of animals were taken entirely by stalking them. I used mostly Kodachrome II films, except for a few rolls of Kodachrome X,

'a slim sixty-four-foot-high tower'
(the hide opposite the bateleur eagle's nest described on page 104)

which I was able to get, and which came in very useful after 6 p.m. when the light began to fade.

I spent altogether three months in Kenya, and wish that I had spent longer in order to get better pictures. I am very grateful to the game wardens such as Larry Wateridge and Rodney Elliott who gave me their unstinting help at the various parks and reserves which I visited; and also to 'Punch' Bearcroft, the plane pilot who helped me with my aerial pictures of flamingos, elephants and other animals. My most grateful thanks, of course, go to Malcolm, who invited me to visit Kenya, and whose faith in my photography encouraged me to achieve the results which you see.

CHRISTINA LOKE

Treasure of Kenya

It took me ten minutes to drive from Government House in Nairobi to visit my neighbours in the near-by National Park. No man could have more congenial neighbours. One of their endearing qualities is that their company is a refreshing relief from the society of human beings. However lovable and glorious the species *Homo sapiens* may be in many of his (and her) characteristics and achievements, certain aspects of mankind's affairs are petty, not to say deplorable; and it is pleasant to view periodically the simpler and to some extent better ordered way of life of the other animals who share with us our occupation of the Earth. Incidentally, their right to continue sharing that planet with us is the principal plea of this book.

So every now and then I went to call on my neighbours in the Nairobi National Park. That distinguished suburb of Kenya's capital stretches across forty-four square miles, and its residents are families of ostriches, herds of giraffes, prides of lions, cohorts of zebras, flocks of storks, a school of hippopotamuses, and teeming companies of scores of other species of wild animals. Only elephants are missing among the larger types of African beasts, and they can be found in abundance elsewhere in Kenya. The place is in some ways like a vast zoological garden—with one significant difference. In it the relationship between Man and his fellow creatures is the reverse of what is usual in such gardens. In Nairobi's park the leopards, baboons, crocodiles, antelopes and other untamed creatures are free to roam at random wherever they wish, and only men are confined in cages.

It is true that those cages are mobile on wheels, for human visitors to the park can drive in motor cars wherever they please. But they are forbidden to emerge from their cars. Nevertheless, they can observe the animals quite closely. For example, they can steer their vehicles to within a few feet of a pride of lions, and park beside those kings of beasts as they sun themselves in the grass. The surprising fact is that you can approach almost as near to a live lion in any of Kenya's nature reserves as you can to one of the artificial lions in Trafalgar Square in London. Usually these genuine African specimens continue to sit as unconcerned as do their images beneath Nelson's Column, eyeing you with indifference as you take their photographs, and perhaps making a concession to the camera by giving a yawn of utter boredom into its lens. But the law of the park strictly decrees that you must stay imprisoned in your car—and woe betide you if you break the law. The lions' unconcern would probably then abruptly cease, and you might not live to tell the tale.

It is similar with all the wild animals everywhere throughout Kenya's game reserves. They are free to wander at will in God's fresh air enjoying all the amenities of bounteous Nature. In these uninhibited zoos only men are confined. I for one find that a welcome reversal of the usual custom in menageries.

The existence of multitudes of varied species of untamed beasts and birds in their

'eyeing you with indifference as you take their photographs'

natural surroundings is not only one of Kenya's finest treasures, but also a precious treasure belonging to the whole world. Save for a few regions in some other parts of Africa such an abundant heritage of beautiful wild life remains nowhere else on Earth. On other continents it has been squandered and largely destroyed. If it is allowed to perish in Africa too, one of the great glories of our planet will be lost for ever—and I do not believe we shall find any satisfactory substitute for it on the Moon, on Venus, Jupiter or Mars, among the myriad stars along the Milky Way, or upon any other new world that Man may discover during the adventurous jaunts on which he is about to embark throughout the Universe.

Yet the preservation of this treasure in Kenya and neighbouring lands is now endangered. That is a threat which should arouse concern among all Mankind.

II

The story of the development of the threat is interesting. A thousand years ago infinite numbers of most of the animal species in evolved Creation roamed freely through nearly all Africa. At that time the only men who hunted them were simple Bushmen and similar nomadic tribes seeking meat and skins. Later Hamitic, Bantu and other native pastoralists and cultivators began to interfere to some extent with the animals' existence; but the toll of life which all those early peoples took was extremely limited. It is true that other hunters

14

existed in the forms of some of the wild beasts themselves, for lions, leopards, cheetahs and other predators lived by devouring certain types of their fellow creatures. But Nature arranged that the victims were only a tiny fraction of their species' grand totals, and that the losses were always adequately replaced. Only great natural upheavals or calamities like earthquakes occasionally exterminated this or that ancient species.

Such destruction had occurred on a vast scale sometimes in much earlier ages, when numerous prehistoric types were for some reason overwhelmed. Fossilised remains of those animals have lain buried in various corners of Kenya and other parts of Africa through countless succeeding millennia; and they are now being dug up in astonishing quantities. Their almost unbelievable forms and varieties present a dramatic picture of the Earth's population a few million years ago. They include not only such titans as elephants, rhinoceroses, ostriches, baboons and other ancestors of present-day species much huger than their still surviving descendants, but also tiny caterpillars, beetles, moths and other insects almost exactly identical with their related types today. Among them, too, are such extraordinary creatures as giraffes with tall branching antlers like Highland stags, pigs with curving canines as formidable as a mastodon's tusks, and pigmy as well as giant forms of several modern creatures. Contemporary with those animals lived Man's own sub-human ancestors, fossilised bits and pieces of whose skeletons are now being unearthed in places like Olduvai Gorge in Tanzania and Fort Ternan in Kenya by those two very distinguished individuals among their eventual progeny, Dr. Louis Leakey and his wife Mary. I have never spent a more interesting morning than my first visit to the Leakeys at Olduvai, when in a three hours tour through the gorge we travelled two million years. Their work seems likely to establish firmly that *Homo sapiens* evolved first in eastern Africa—a historical probability which makes their digging sites treasure-houses even more precious to Kenya's and Tanzania's prestige than gold-mines, diamond mines or oil-wells.

But I must not wander in these pages into those diverting fields. Let me return to the subject of Kenya's present-day living animals.

In early historical times there was some interference with Africa's fauna by men outside Africa. Thus, just as Stone Age men in Europe had killed local mammoths, extracted their tusks, and engraved vivid sketches on them, so also in antique Egypt, archaic and classical Greece, and ancient Rome ivory was in considerable demand for carving *objets d'art*. The raw material was taken mostly from African elephants. Incidentally, the elephants with which Hannibal crossed the Alps were chiefly north African monsters. But again, the numbers of animals destroyed or captured for such purposes were negligible.

Then European and Asian exploitation of African resources began in greater earnest, especially along the largely unexplored continent's lengthy coasts. But still the depredations of wild life by the natives in the interior and by those foreigners along the edges of the land were in no sense formidable. Even though the trade in elephant tusks, and later in rhinoceros horn—which for some odd reason acquired among Oriental peoples, and especially the Chinese, an undeserved reputation for magical aphrodisiac qualities—encouraged the slaughter of those beasts on an increasing scale, the supply of them stayed far in excess of

15

the demand. Africa continued to be a teeming paradise for countless species of animals, some of their herds swarming here, there and everywhere in millions.

Then, a few centuries ago, Europeans started permanent agricultural settlements in southern Africa; and the picture began to change. Unbridled hunting of wild game began to reduce significantly the numbers of various species, and to lead towards even the complete extinction of certain types in the affected area. Various reasons prompted this, the main one being that the farmers naturally needed the land for grazing their flocks and herds, and they did not wish rivals in the form of antelopes and other wild herbivores to stay around. So first the regions near the southernmost tip of Africa, and then gradually others stretching northwards to the Orange River, became increasingly deprived of vast throngs of free-roaming untamed beasts. As an example, before the city of Johannesburg was founded men recorded that close-packed herds of springbok stretching half-a-mile wide and taking several hours to run past a given spot were common on its site; but these were afterwards massacred in hundreds of thousands. The floral destruction was as massive as that among the fauna; and many types of indigenous African plants have disappeared for ever from the face of the Earth.

For a long time an unexpected circumstance prevented the extension of this change further north. When the farmers tried to push their areas of settlement beyond a certain region they met a formidable enemy. It was not embattled native tribesmen, nor hosts of man-eating lions, nor unconquerable armies of other hostile beasts, nor the obstinate opposition of an arid desert, but a tiny flying insect called the tsetse fly. Existing in swarming multitudes, it dealt out death to domestic oxen, horses and other unaccustomed creatures, and made human farming virtually impossible. Even the long-accustomed native herds of cattle and goats succumbed to the fatal disease it carried, and as a result those herds only survived in severely limited quantities in strictly confined places. Some species of the fly bore the germs of an illness—sleeping sickness—which was mortal to men themselves; and in areas where they thrived the human population, too, was almost non-existent.

Yet the tsetse fly had no ill effects whatever on any of the wild animals indigenous to Africa. They were immune to its wicked sting; and so they continued to live and roam with impunity throughout most of the continent. Other creatures may be more grand or beautiful, or in other ways admirable than the tsetse; but in the history of Africa this little insect (generally about the size of a house-fly) is by far the most important character. Among other achievements, until the latest few decades it was the hero who unwittingly preserved Africa's treasure of wild life.

In the latter half of the nineteenth century, however, intrepid European explorers began to intrude ever further into Africa's interior. Because of the ravages wrought by tsetse flies among cattle and horses, they could not take caravans of pack-animals with them, and had to use small armies of load-carrying porters instead. They were soon followed by representatives of Humanity's conscience seeking to abolish the slave trade which for generations had flourished throughout those regions. Later came British, German and other Colonial

Governments, bringing with them modern medicine, veterinary services, scientific research, and other sophisticated powers which started to alter the whole situation. The assaults of human diseases were countered, and so the native African populations increased quite rapidly; the tsetse flies' depredations were first checked and then reduced, with the result that herds of domestic cattle and goats multiplied; and, since among many tribes ownership of cattle was the symbol of wealth, the numbers of cows and bulls were soon allowed to increase far beyond judicious proportions. To maintain them wide new areas of land were required for domestic grazing; and partly because cattle are considerably less economical in their consumption of grasses than are antelopes and other similar herbivores, much territory became incapable of supporting both the earlier and the new animal populations. Wild beasts were forced to retreat before the civilised invasion. That situation was aggravated when white farmers as well as white hunters came in large numbers to settle in congenial parts of the freshly opened country, and when railways, commerce, and business enterprises established towns and cities here and there, spreading tentacles of communications and transport across ever-widening regions. At the same time not only hunting for sport, but also poaching for ivory, horn, skins and other trophies with a trading value increased many-fold—and the chief victims of all these revolutionary changes were (apart from the tsetse fly) the colossal herds of wildebeests, zebras, elephants, rhinoceroses, giraffes, ostriches, lions, and other beasts which hitherto had owned almost the whole continent.

I need not recount the story in detail. A few generations ago those animals used to move in millions across the vast land, and even one generation ago there were a hundred times the numbers that exist today. The threat to the survivors continues in spite of the belated establishment of national parks, game reserves and other protective controls in certain regions. Within more or less recent decades several additional unique species have become extinct—such as the Barbary lion, the Cape quagga, the Atlas bear, and the South African blue-buck—and additional species are now on the danger list, like the white rhinoceros and the black rhinoceros. The loss to the variety and beauty of Nature in the world is deplorable, and may become irretrievably disastrous. The treasure is being spent at a spendthrift rate. Unless adequate restorative action is taken quickly, all action will be too late.

III

In spite of the depredations that I have mentioned, the variety of wild life in Kenya's nature reserves is still very remarkable. When I arrived in Nairobi as Governor in January 1963 I did not expect to have much opportunity to view it. So many difficult and urgent political, constitutional and administrative problems had to be overcome as quickly as possible that I thought I would spend all the time working with herds of Ministers and officials, and find no leisure for play with herds of zebras and gnus. During the first three months that was indeed the case. All day and every day Mr. Jomo Kenyatta, Mr. Ronald

Ngala, their KANU and KADU colleagues, and I and my advisers were toiling so continuously at tasks preparatory to Kenya's Independence that we scarcely had time to go to bed, let alone to go on safari.

Then a most fortunate accident happened to me. I was viciously assaulted by a pneumonia bug. And that stroke of good luck was followed by another. The doctors suspected that my pneumonia was complicated by a weak heart condition; and as a result of that double frailty they ordered me away from Nairobi for several weeks of strict convalescence. I was to do no work, to see no official persons, to read no newspapers, to write no letters, to think no political thoughts, and to do virtually nothing. When I asked whether I might go and spend the time with more or less dumb animals like elephants and giraffes who never read newspapers, never listened to the radio, never made speeches, and never gave a thought to Kenya's politics, my medical advisers thought this a permissible idea.

So I went on a series of expeditions under the guidance of such devoted and knowledgeable nature lovers as Larry Wateridge in Mara, Bill Langridge in Amboseli and Tsavo, Chris Megson at Kiboko, David Roberts at Baringo, Rodney Elliott in Maralal, and Freddie Seed beside the Uaso Nyiro river. When I returned to Nairobi six weeks later my pneumonia bug was stone dead, and my heart was very much alive and kicking. On further consideration the doctors decided that there had never been anything radically wrong with the latter item.

The results for me were many unforgettable glimpses of the wild life still to be seen in Kenya's nature reserves. Let me hint at its variety by mentioning the creatures which I saw during one late afternoon jaunt lasting little more than an hour in a land-rover at Mara. They included a herd of about 300 buffalo, and later a party of three particularly tough-looking bulls of that breed; four separate groups of impala, the largest of which contained one lordly ram with his harem of some forty ewes; a solitary old tusker elephant; a company of forty-two giraffes, and afterwards another party of six of those peripatetic Eiffel towers; a troop of more than sixty massive elands; a frisky pair of little dik-diks; several cohorts of zebras totalling a few hundred beasts altogether; considerably larger herds of Grant's gazelles and Thomson's gazelles; wildebeests galore; half-a-dozen hartebeests; several small groups of topis; a trio of warthogs; a couple of jackals playing with their twin half-grown cubs; and a lone spotted hyena. The list of birds was even longer, including a quartet of ostriches, a flock of twenty-six crowned cranes feeding together on a swarm of grasshoppers, a hammerkop, a bateleur eagle, a tawny eagle, three other species of birds of prey, and more than two dozen different types of smaller birds. All these diverse animals were congregated within a distance of a few miles; and many of them were very unshy, being accustomed to regard a stray land-rover as just some species of armour-plated monster like a rhinoceros sharing with them their homeland. The giraffes, for example, did not lollop away at their customary graceful canter when I drove within fifteen yards of them, but stood and gazed down at me with mild, condescending curiosity as I passed.

I came upon the solitary spotted hyena towards dusk. It, too, showed aloof indifference

'a herd of about 300 buffalo'

when my car drove near. Its furtive eyes were watching with interested concentration some incident occurring a mile or two away across the plain; and after casting a momentary disapproving glance towards me as I approached—as if to whisper 'Go away!'—its gaze at once reverted to whatever scene fascinated it there. I suspected that it had sighted a lion or leopard starting its evening hunt, and that the hyena was waiting hopefully to spy a kill which it could later scavenge when the king or prince of beasts had feasted. Next afternoon I therefore went in the direction of the hyena's gaze; and, sure enough, I found not just one lion loitering there, but the handsomest pride of lions I have ever seen. The party consisted of four well-maned males, seven lionesses, and three small cubs. Herds of zebras, wildebeests and gazelles were grazing in the vicinity in full view of that leonine group, all feeding relaxedly, unperturbed by the mighty hunters' presence. Evidently the hyena's hope of the previous evening had been fulfilled: the lions had stalked successfully, slain a victim, and gorged themselves so that their hunger was satisfied for at least a day or two. Their possible next victims instinctively knew this, and felt safe. A rhinoceros roaming in the neighbourhood was even more carefree, since it did not in any case fear a mere dozen lions.

'Christina Loke had come to stay with us'

Mara is a game reserve in Masailand, a vast area of undisturbed, unspoilt country twice the size of Wales where that proud pastoralist tribe, the Masai, are the human lords and masters. My wife Audrey and I had our first glimpse of true African Nature there when we took our friend Christina Loke—who had come to stay with us to make the illustrations for this book—on our first Kenya safari. Under the guidance of that most eminent of all game wardens, Major Lyn Temple-Boreham, we motored morning, afternoon and evening along primitive rural tracks where the wild country from horizon to horizon appeared as if it had been virtually untouched since the beginning of Time. Spacious landscapes of open plains and smooth hills with scatterings of bushes and trees succeeded each other all day long. There I felt more strongly than on any other continent the immense age of this Earth; and I became aware of the abiding elemental character of Africa in particular. Nowhere else in the world can one feel so limitlessly free in wide open spaces. That Mara scenery had unbounded beauty. Every now and then large herds of wild beasts wandered as of right across the land, appearing much as they might have done at any time in the last million years. And just occasionally we met small parties of some half-a-dozen Masai warriors, looking like children of Adam as they strode forward with athletic, near-naked, ebony-black bodies adorned only by their ornamental hair-dos, red robes thrown loosely across their shoulders, and long spears held ready for action.

20

IV

Somewhat similar impressions greet visitors in all Kenya's national parks and game reserves. They lurk not only throughout the forty-four square miles of Nairobi's park, and the 700 square miles in the Mara Reserve, but also across 1,260 square miles at Amboseli, 800 square miles in the preserve around Marsabit, 8,034 square miles at Tsavo, 228 square miles encircling Mount Kenya, 400 square miles in the Meru Reserve, and through several other similarly spacious wild estates elsewhere. Inside them wild animals are protected; no one can shoot, snare or trap them. They roam at complete liberty. Even domestic cattle and goats are forbidden to intrude into nearly all those kingdoms of the beasts, because their grazing and browsing of local supplies of vegetation would prejudice the chances of survival of their untamed brethren. Native cattle and goats can go to grass in next-door areas, where in other ways, too, creatures like elephants, lions, leopards and rhinoceroses lack full protection. In those places so-called sportsmen can buy licences to shoot certain numbers of various types of game. But all the national parks and reserves are sacrosanct against such killings.

One of the most rewarding of them for visitors is the reserve at Amboseli, lying along Kenya's southern border with Tanzania. In addition to other attractions, the landscapes there are majestic because the back-drop to almost every scene is Mount Kilimanjaro. Rising in dramatic loneliness from the surrounding plains, with a near-symmetrical cone-shaped form reminiscent of Japan's immaculate Fujiyama, the old volcano rears its hefty yet graceful bulk to a height of more than 19,000 feet. Although it stands almost on the Equator, and its lower slopes are for ever green or blue according to the vagaries of the atmosphere, its peak sparkles white with eternal snows. Sometimes the mountain shrouds itself in mist, but as frequently it reveals every inch of its imposing figure gleaming in the sunlight beneath a cloudless sky.

On its summit strange gods were alleged to live; and round its foot wander elephants, lions, giraffes, ostriches and all sorts of other gracious creatures, like courtiers attending a durbar of those gods. They swarm everywhere through the surrounding country, which is a mixture of broad open plains, bush-studded savannah, denser forest, and rock-strewn hills, with an occasional splash of a small lake. Camera enthusiasts will be interested to learn the variety of different animals which Chris Loke photographed on a six days expedition which a party of us made there. Let me set them down in the order in which she captured their portraits. Naturally the list contains several repetitions, for sometimes second or third opportunities to get pictures of this or that species offered better poses than the earlier chances.

On the first day Chris took photographs of the impala, lilac-breasted roller, superb starling, white-bearded wildebeest, cattle egret, saddle-bill stork, Burchell's zebra, Masai giraffe, common waterbuck, sacred ibis, long-toed plover, blacksmith plover, black rhinoceros, ox-pecker, lion, African jacana, black crake, black-shouldered kite, black-headed heron, and yellow-necked spurfowl.

On the second day her bag included the kori bustard, black-headed heron, impala, vervet monkey, white-browed coucal, elephant, Thomson's gazelle, Burchell's zebra, Masai giraffe, Egyptian goose, blacksmith plover, black rhinoceros, hippopotamus, square-marked toad, and cricket.

On the third morning the list had reached Egyptian goose, Goliath heron, wood sandpiper, reeve, sacred ibis, long-toed plover and blacksmith plover by eleven o'clock, when a storm of rain descended and sent us trundling helter-skelter in our land-rover back to the comfort of our camp. The sky cleared after lunch, and we sallied forth again to spend a long time getting good pictures of a pair of blacksmith plovers incubating eggs on their nest. Then we secured more snapshots of a reeve and a wood sandpiper before finishing up with a buffalo.

On the fourth day Chris's camera caught the white pelican, pink-backed pelican, white-bearded wildebeest, fringe-eared oryx, gerenuk, ostrich and lion.

On the fifth she took photographs of the helmeted guinea-fowl, white-bearded wildebeest, spurwing goose, Egyptian goose, redbilled teal, blacksmith plover, Thomson's gazelle, black-headed heron, little grebe, two-banded courser, white-faced tree duck, wigeon, great white egret, squacco heron, grey heron, elephant, wattled starling, crowned plover, bat-eared fox, lion, white-bellied bustard, saddle-bill stork, vervet monkey, cheetah, grey hornbill, and Masai giraffe.

By then she had photographed, I had scribbled notes about, and Bill Langridge had recorded the voices of, a gratifying variety of species, and we tried to be more particular in our selection. We were especially keen to find a leopard. Soon after sunrise the next morning we therefore set forth to track one of those lovely, elusive cats—and at about four o'clock in the afternoon we added its picture to our portrait gallery. But in the meantime the indefatigable camera-woman had been diverted by other passers-by striking attitudes too tempting to be ignored; and she had devoted films to the Masai giraffe, superb starling, vervet monkey, white-browed coucal, impala, common waterbuck, go-away bird, black rhinoceros, chestnut-bellied sandgrouse, eight or nine different species of herons, egrets, geese and wild duck bathing in a pool, the spotted hyena, white-bellied bustard, silver-backed jackal, and baboon.

Before we left Amboseli early the next morning she spent an hour snapping the ring-necked dove, superb starling, long-tailed fiscal shrike, Reichenow's weaver, and white stork. In six days and a fragment of a seventh she had taken more than 1,500 pictures of sixty-four different species of birds and beasts—not to mention an occasional study also of three sub-species of the order *Homo sapiens* in the forms of Masai warriors, Kipsigis game-scouts, and European tourists.

In addition to the animals which she photographed we saw various other types each and every day; but there was only time to pick and choose a selection from all the possible models parading before her camera and our field-glasses. Sometimes we stayed more or less motionless for hours on end whilst she waited patiently for this or that desirable creature to strike the right pose in the correct conditions for a good portrait, and during

'a herd of elephants'

those periods she had no eyes for any other candidates, however photogenic they might be. For example, one afternoon we spent three hours following a herd of more than a hundred elephants in the hope that they would present her with some classic pictures. They were a grand mixed company of old bulls, younger bulls, cows, and calves of all ages; and they cooperated with us well as they ambled across the scene. But the sun and clouds were very uncooperative. Almost all the time the former was hiding behind the latter, and occasionally light rain floated down, with negative results so far as first-class colour photography was concerned.

V

One of the enchanting aspects of such expeditions into Kenya's wilds is the constant element of surprise which attends them. A traveller never knows what species of animals he will meet at any moment on any day. For example, at crack of dawn one morning we set forth to secure pictures of that graceful if slightly grotesque antelope, the gerenuk. We drove for more than an hour to a remote corner of the reserve where we were told we would have the best chance of achieving our aim. Indeed, we were assured that the chance was a certainty, since the locality was plentifully scattered with the tall bushes on which gerenuks like to feed, and several parties of those antelopes had been seen there during the preceding days. When we arrived, however, the whole region seemed empty of animal life. It was a vast plain of bushland pimpled here and there by a high hillock from which we could get clear views from one horizon to another; but when we climbed those prominences and scanned the landscapes, no gerenuk was anywhere in sight. After wide reconnaissances we abandoned hope, and returned to less likely areas in search of other game. We felt frustrated, for gerenuks are especially coveted models for photography.

On our outward journey we had received one unexpected reward by getting shots of a beautiful flock of pink-backed and white pelicans on a reflective sheet of water where an ornithological member of our team declared that they had never been seen before. Now we received another reward in the congenial shape of a herd of fringe-eared oryx which behaved much less shyly than most of their kind, giving us opportunities for excellent camera studies. In addition we met a picturesque party of young Masai warriors strolling across the country with their long spears held in readiness for imaginary battles.

Arriving back in regions much less agreeable to our desired gerenuks, we dismissed those animals from our minds and concentrated on other species. There was a goodly herd of white-bearded wildebeests attended by a flock of cattle egrets, which is one of the many pleasant, mutually beneficial associations of birds and beasts in such places. We took many pictures of them. Then we came across a spectacular family of ostriches consisting of a father, a mother and thirty-one identical three-quarters grown youngsters—like a litter of twins, triplets, quadruplets, etc. *ad infinitum*. They strolled in procession with the cock leading, followed by all the offspring and with the matronly hen bringing up the rear. We were carefully manoeuvring our land-rover into position to get interesting photographs of that charming pageant—when two gerenuks strode in front of us as if they had just arrived from nowhere!

They appeared unconcerned by our proximity, and started to feed on near-by bushes. The chance of getting shots of them was too good to be missed, especially as some of the shrubs were tall, and one or other of the antelopes might therefore perform its graceful act of rising on its hind-legs, balancing like a ballet dancer on tip-toe, and nibbling with upstretched neck and head at succulent leaves on a bush-top. In any case we knew that the ostriches would not stray far away, and that we could easily get pictures of them afterwards.

So for the next hour we attended upon the two gerenuks; and one of them collaborated with us to perfection. It performed its ballet *pas seul* at just the right distance from our seats in the land-rover, enabling Chris to make as fine a set of pictures of the lovely antelope as have ever been taken. Some of them appear later in this book.

Having gained that supreme—and at the time unexpected—object, we turned to secure photographs of the ostrich family. Providence, however, is not usually over-indulgent in her bestowal of gifts. The thirty-three grand birds had strolled only a few hundred yards away, where they still displayed themselves in very photogenic array. But as we turned our land-rover in their direction, and advanced towards a clearing where we could get admirable shots of them, one of our car-wheels blew a puncture. Whilst we were still repairing it ten minutes later the hitherto brilliant sun disappeared behind late afternoon clouds—and it never re-emerged from them.

VI

The day when we set forth dedicated to the task of finding a leopard was another typical experience. Of all the wild African cats the leopard is perhaps the most difficult to photograph, for it is uncommon, shy, and wary. By contrast the photography of lions is child's play, for that ferocious beast poses for its portrait as readily as any other monarch on parade before a crowd of newspaper cameramen. The cheetah, on the other hand, is more elusive and cautious, whilst such night prowlers as civets and serval cats are very hard to come by. But most uncooperative of all is the leopard. Except for a single specimen in Tanzania's Serengeti Park which has been nicknamed 'Good as Gold' because it will often climb a tree and sit sunning itself, as good as gold, on a convenient branch whilst tourists take snapshots of it, I have heard of no member of the tribe which does not strongly object to any such liberties.

Nevertheless we felt reasonably optimistic that morning, for we were guided to an area where an adult female leopard with her cub had been observed several times during the two previous days. We expected to catch at least a glimpse of them. But when we reached the promised land there was no sign of the couple. As usual, all sorts of other creatures diverted us instead, many of them presenting views of themselves which were too tempting for us students of Nature to resist. Having started on our leopard hunt at 7.30 a.m., we had taken photographs of, and scribbled notes on, more than a score of other species by mid-afternoon.

At 3.30 p.m. we were observing a merry party of baboons consisting of a dozen elders and youngsters. Three 'teenage'-looking brats were at delightful play. One performed a hesitant but deliberate series of cartwheels; a second seemed to be trying to stand on its head; and the third endeavoured to distract the others' attention to a game of touch-last. The trio kept whirling, tumbling and darting around like a team of acrobats practising for a circus turn. Then one of them walked to a stone, squatted on it with statuesque immobility, and assumed a look of absorbed innocence as if its thoughts were far away, like those of a meditative Indian holy-man forgetful of this mischievous world. One of its companions thereupon crept stealthily towards it from behind—and as soon as that intruder came near it the statue woke into instant life, leaped into the air, and did a sort of backwards somersault over its companion's head. The couple repeated the action three times in succession, as if they were rehearsing the act for faultless performance later on a stage. Then they closed in a mock wrestling match, and their third colleague was on the point of joining them—when they, and we, were disturbed by a sudden loud chattering of vervet monkeys about a hundred yards away.

'Tchui!' muttered our African game-scout sitting in the land-rover, speaking Swahili.

'Leopard!' translated Bill Langridge waiting alert at the steering-wheel.

25

He started the engine, and we left the baboons to their fun whilst we proceeded cautiously in the direction of the vervets' hullabaloo. As we approached we heard ever more loudly a frenzied chorus of coughing, scolding and gibbering coming from a group of tree-tops. Monkeys often work themselves into such excitement at a glimpse of a leopard, for that expert hunter is their deadliest enemy.

Soon we came in sight of a dozen vervets sitting near the ends of high branches in a circle of trees, all staring earthwards towards the same central spot, like spectators in the gallery seats overlooking an arena. By following their gaze we could tell where the leopard crouched, concealed in a clump of bushes.

As Chris set her camera on its swivelling clamp fixed in one of the car's window spaces, light rain began to fall—the first shower after more than three days of unblemished sunshine! We halted the vehicle, and concentrated our scrutiny on the group of shrubs, not blinking an eyelid and scarcely daring to draw breath. Our view-point was evidently not so advantageous as that of the monkeys, for we could detect no sign whatever of a feline figure, a patch of spotted coat, or any furtive movement among the thick foliage; whereas they probably had an excellent sight of their foe, for they maintained a vehement shindy of protests.

For a quarter of an hour—which seemed like several hours—we waited motionless. Then the demonstrators in the tree-tops worked themselves into a crescendo of fury, and a moment later we caught sight of a leopard emerging from the furthest extremity of the bushes, and walking with slow, nonchalant dignity across an open space. Perhaps it sensed our presence, for after a minute it suddenly leapt into hiding in another patch of shrubbery. But we had seen enough to know that it was a solitary, nearly full-grown youngster.

Very cautiously, and as quietly as possible, we followed it in our vehicle, and stopped at a discreet distance from its new retreat. For a while we saw nothing there except a tangle of tall grasses, much bushy foliage, and some broken tree-stumps and branches jutting from the undergrowth. Then a slight movement revealed to us the spotted cat's lovely face contemplating us from a hollow in the ground beneath a tumbled tree-trunk. Its gaze was inquisitive, serene and self-confident.

Fortunately the rain had ceased as suddenly as it started. At the sound of Chris's camera shutter snapping a portrait (reproduced opposite page 176) the leopard stirred, looked around calmly for an exit by which it could escape, insinuated itself noiselessly through a space below the fallen tree, and as silently as a shadow disappeared from our view. Soon afterwards we saw its whole body emerge from a patch of bracken ten yards further away, and start to stroll across a wide stretch of open ground. Once more its audience of excited monkeys raised their voices in furious scolding; and they followed its course by agitated hops-skips-and-jumps from branch to branch among the lofty trees as it proceeded. It paid no heed to them, neither looking up to observe them, nor hastening its leisurely steps. Nor did it so much as acknowledge our presence by a passing glance at us. With superb grace of movement, and with an air of fearless mastery of all it surveyed, it walked a hundred yards across the ground. Then at the sound of our land-rover's engine starting up again it recovered its shy wildness, and trotted into another clump of bushes.

In their midst stood a tall, broken tree-stump. We saw the leopard raise itself on its hind-legs against the trunk, stretch its fore-paws on to the bark and scratch them a few times, as if it were sharpening its claws. For a while it seemed to be debating with itself whether to climb the broken tree and take a view of the world from its summit; but then it decided against the idea, and slunk into the undergrowth.

For half an hour we and the monkeys lay in wait for its reappearance; but in vain. After that the monkeys lost interest, descended from their tree-tops, and scampered away across the ground in pursuit of other diversions. We waited for yet another half-hour; but again with no results. Whether the leopard had secretly left its concealment, observed by the monkeys when they became reassured, or whether it still lay doggo in the bushes, and they had merely become bored, we never knew. The episode was a brilliant example of a leopard's capacity to disappear into thin air.

VII

One of the impressive features of all that wild life is the free and mutually tolerant manner in which many different species of animals usually associate together. This is in spite of the fact that some of them are recognised predators who periodically chase and kill members of other breeds in their locality. Thus, although such giants as elephants, rhinoceroses, hippopotamuses and giraffes are vegetarians who never do harm (except occasionally in self-defence) to any fellow creature, other masterful beasts like lions, leopards and cheetahs are carnivores who live by consuming goodly numbers of their neighbours. However, those murderous characters kill only for essential eating, not for mere 'sport' or the love of killing; and they require food only at certain intervals. A good square meal consumed by a lion, for example, satisfies it for two, three or more days; and during the intervening period it does not need to hunt. Its neighbours of other species, including its favourite dishes like zebras and wildebeests, know by instinct or shrewd observation when the hunter is replete, and also when it is growing hungry again; and throughout the former interludes they show no sign of nervousness, grazing apparently carefree in the close vicinity of their potential destroyer. Naturally the prospective victims always keep a wary eye, ear or nostril open, some of them detecting the approach of danger chiefly by sight, others by hearing, and yet others by smell; and often they have an organised system of sentinels which gives them warning of any likely attack.

In the same way the prey of other killers recognise their murderers, and seek to maintain a prudent avoidance of them, whether those enemies live on the ground like wild dogs and hyenas, or in the air like eagles, hawks and owls. But the would-be victims cannot always keep on the alert, and so much of the time they appear indifferent. As a result the great

27

'small creatures like . . . chameleons'

mixture of varied birds and beasts in Africa's wild society generally give an impression of observing peaceful co-existence. How unpeaceful that existence is in fact is obvious when one recollects that large hunters like lions and eagles are not the only animals who live by eating their fellow-beings. Small creatures like toads, lizards, chameleons, starlings, warblers, thrushes and a myriad others conduct a perpetual warfare against insects, worms, grubs and suchlike victims. In addition fishermen like storks, pelicans and herons swallow large quantities of aquatic animals, whilst some of those inhabitants of water conduct a ceaseless campaign against one another. Yet the casualties suffered in all that constant struggle account for only small fractions of the total contemporary populations of the innumerable species involved; and so for the overwhelming majority of each and all of them the apparent fact of peaceful co-existence is not too much of an illusion.

As a result a visitor to the wild life reserves in Kenya can see astonishing multitudes of different animals associating peacefully together. Thus I spent one afternoon and night in the famous retreat called 'Treetops' in the Aberdare National Park, where Her Majesty Queen Elizabeth II was staying when her father died and she ascended the throne. During those hours I saw waterbucks, bushbucks, elephants, warthogs, giant forest hogs, baboons, buffaloes, rhinoceroses, wild ducks, geese, storks, ibises, waders, egrets and other beasts

28

and birds mixing together in various groups in perfect harmony around the salt-lick below the hotel's verandah. They strolled about in close view of each other, and often intermingled with mutual tolerance. The only hint of a possible rivalry was when a huge tusker elephant and a heftily horned rhinoceros eyed each other uncertainly, advanced towards one another suspiciously, and engaged in a brief mock duel of hostile passes with their respective weapons. But they soon parted without any actual conflict. The only physical contacts between any of the animals were interlockings of trunks by elephants exchanging friendly greetings. During the afternoon half-a-dozen separate herds of those giants converged on the salt-lick, until as many as 140 grand jumbos were assembled there together. Often when a new party arrived an individual from an earlier group would step out to salute one of the latest comers. With seeming affection both elephants raised their long trunks towards each other, interwove them round one another, and even clashed tusks in a gentle, mutually appreciative sort of way. Sometimes between a male and a female the contact was rather different. The bull would lay its trunk lengthways along the cow's back, possibly with a suggestion of solicitation. But the gesture was momentary, fleeting—perhaps to be repeated later with greater insistence in more auspicious surroundings. Many young elephants of various ages and sizes were also in the herds, and they often gave fond strokes with their miniature trunks to their elders' flanks and legs. Every now and then the tiniest of them, a calf only one month old, sauntered beneath its mother's stomach, tucked its trunk out of the way, and sucked with its mouth at her teats near her fore-legs.

Such remarkable, mixed, peaceful associations of many different sorts of animals could be quoted from countless occasions in numerous places in my experience. Indeed, to a regular visitor to Kenya's national parks they cease to be remarkable at all, and express the ordinary, normal way of life of their wild populations. In particular, teeming herds of zebras, wildebeests and other kinds of antelopes often intermingle together, with ostriches, giraffes and occasional warthogs keeping them company.

Similar mixtures are as common on water as on land. I remember the company one afternoon at Mzima Springs in Tsavo Park. In the middle of the pool twenty hippopotamuses wallowed contentedly up to their eyes, ears and snouts under water. Twenty yards away three crocodiles lazed in the shallows, one with its mouth wide open in what appeared to be a perpetual petrified yawn. Close beside it a Goliath heron stood fishing, whilst on a nearby fallen tree-trunk a pair of darters perched with their wings outstretched to dry, looking like heraldic birds. Occasionally a kingfisher hovered in the air above them before turning a somersault and plunging into the depths. A group of vervet monkeys occupied tree-tops overlooking the pool, some of them sitting motionless in contemplative mood, others busily de-bugging each others' furry coats, and yet others ceaselessly gambolling as they strolled on all fours along branches, swung upside-down beneath the boughs, or played a game of touch-last in and out and round about among the foliage. On the river bank a ram impala and his harem were serenely grazing; round the water's edge coots, moorhens, crakes and bitterns hunted their respective preys; near the centre of the pool a cormorant was cruising and diving after eels below; and no doubt in the submarine world all manner of fish swam in shoals. The dominant characters in the scene were the hefty hippopotamuses and crocodiles, but occasionally a melodious snatch of song from an oriole overhead indicated that Beauty as well as the Beast was attending the party.

In wholly avian society a similar situation prevails. Nowhere is the general peaceful co-existence of wild-bird life more evident than on the series of lakes poured along the floor of the Great Rift Valley. Consider Lake Nakuru, for example. In human society such tremendous multitudes of individuals as gather there never congregate even on such massive occasions as a cup-final football match in London, a fraternal Communist rally in Peking, or a Christmas Eve shopping spree in New York. At seasons when flamingoes are in occupation of the place I have seen nearly two millions of those fabulously graceful creatures wading in the shallows, swimming on the depths, and flying through the air. They jam-pack confined areas of the water like demonstrators marshalled to espouse some passionate political cause. Nor are they alone, for in spaces of water, land and sky between their assemblies float, paddle and fly additional fleets of pelicans, storks, ibises, ducks, geese, egrets, avocets, stilts, gulls, terns, plovers, coots, moorhens, sandpipers, cormorants, darters, cranes, crakes, grebes, and innumerable other species of water and shore birds, with all manner of landlubbing types in the surrounding reed-beds, fields and woods. Expert observers have counted more than 200 different species on a single day's visit to Lake Nakuru. One of the most abiding impressions of those astonishing sights is the complete mutual tolerance, peace and concord in which they all live tumultuously together.

VIII

Night life in the African wilds is as ceaselessly active as is existence throughout the daytime. Many animals sleep at nights and feed during the days; but numerous others reverse that order, dozing in the daylight hours and hunting for food at nights. On even the most casual motor journeys after dark one sees a lot of evidence of that. For example, on a trip from Narok to Nairobi lasting a couple of hours on each side of midnight I caught sight in my car's headlights of many dik-diks and jackals, a duiker, numerous specimens of two different types of nightjars, three different species of owls, countless rabbits and hares, and a civet cat, all on the prowl on the road ahead of me. Occasionally I saw shadowy figures of other creatures such as gazelles, impalas and giraffes strolling past my vehicle's windows; and from the remoter darkness came sounds of yet other beasts attacking their food, like the blood-curdling laughter of hyenas. Many great hunters are most active at nights, such as leopards on the ground and owls in the air.

One of the liveliest and noisiest inhabitants of the tree-tops then is the engaging animal shown opposite, the lesser bush baby. Throughout every day it slumbers in holes in rotten trees or similar resorts, a group of several of them often cuddling together for their sojourn

'the lesser bush baby'

in dreamland. After dusk they emerge for a night's energetic hunting and gambolling. On moonlit evenings in several places in Kenya I have seen parties of half-a-dozen of their silhouettes scampering along branches, and making gigantic jumps from tree to tree as they emitted their excited screams and whistles. About the size of average squirrels, they are pretty, round-eyed, large-eared creatures, who sometimes make charmingly gentle pets. But they can also show sudden bad temper, sinking their sharp teeth at the slightest provocation into an owner's fingers. Those teeth of course do good service, too, in assaults on the insects, berries, fruits, birds' eggs, and nestlings which are the bush baby's customary menu.

The actual individual portrayed here was a semi-domesticated resident of the near-wilds at Kiboko. All day long it slept concealed in a crevice in the ceiling-thatch of the game warden's, Barry Chappell's, round native-style house; but at nights it issued forth, jumped down the wall into the living-room, and spent the evening companionably with Barry and his wife as they sat reading, writing or talking in the lamplight there. When they went to bed it ascended again to the roof beneath the stars, leaped across an astonishingly wide space into a tree, and for the next several hours until daylight joined its own kind in their nightly revels.

31

IX

An engaging, and to a newcomer often surprising feature of all this African wild life is the gentle, affectionate relationship which unites the members of families of the various beasts, including some of the most savage. Among pacific, inoffensive animals like giraffes that is no doubt to be expected; and yet the charm of suddenly coming across a clannish party of those mobile towers browsing in thorn-bush country never loses its element of startlement. The lanky-legged, telescope-necked, pin-headed freaks always appear at first sight unbelievably fabulous. Sometimes I have seen them in companies of forty or more, the individuals attaining various different sizes, but all displaying exactly the same shape. They travel together with an obvious sense of mutual friendship and collective security. Full-grown females in such groups are often attended by their miniature offspring, and the bond of kinship between mother and child is as apparent as in the most closely knit human family. A youngster never strays far from its parent's side, and often it scampers to her, thrusts its head beneath her belly, and starts to refresh itself with her milk.

Similar attachments mark social life among almost all species. Everyone knows that the gruff, powerful-horned buffalo can be as irate and aggressive a beast as any on earth; but a charmingly tender and almost sentimental bond unites the male and the female, the old and the young in a herd. At certain seasons small, recently born calves accompany their elders; and it is impressive to watch the instinctive, natural competence with which those youngsters travel amidst the more mature troop. They keep pace with the adults as they walk, trot or run, maintain their positions whenever the group manoeuvres, never get in the way of grown-up hooves, and usually manage to overcome successfully all the obstacles in their paths. Every now and then, however, one makes a childish error, and immediately a parent or guardian comes to its rescue. For instance, I have watched a herd stampeding through soft mud alongside a river. The older beasts plunged effortlessly through the muck, the quagmire rising only knee-deep for them. But for the calves it squelched belly-high, and they encountered occasional obstructions as they hastened forward. The more adolescent among them managed to advance without too much difficulty, and their particular parents made no attempt to help them, doubtless knowing intuitively that the experience would be good for them in stimulating natural-born skills and self-reliance. But now and then a more infantile youngster met real trouble in extricating itself from a patch of mire— and at once an adult beast would turn to lend it encouragement or aid. Evidently the elders were continuously aware of their juveniles' whereabouts, problems and fortunes amidst the herd. And when actual danger looms—such as when a pride of lions are about to attack— a buffalo troop promptly assumes a defensive formation, the bulls taking up position on the outer flanks to form a shield for the cows, and the cows in their turn protecting the calves, who are chivvied into the centre of the party.

It is similar with elephants. Those hefty yet usually gentle monsters normally travel around in comparatively small parties of one or two dozen; but sometimes several groups combine to form a considerable herd of one or two hundred. These contain a mixture of giants and pigmies, several elephant generations from near-centenarians to few-weeks-old youngsters ambling cheek by jowl, and trunk by tusk, in the company. The veterans will moderate the pace of their progress through the countryside to suit the convenience of the smallest jumbo among them; the mothers are for ever solicitous about the well-being of their infants, feeding, washing, fondling, and when necessary spanking them; and the bulls are always ready to play their part in defending the herd against any interference. Nor are the various parental responsibilities entirely individual matters for each mother or father respectively, but rather collective duties recognised to some extent by the whole group. Thus if one matron dies, a foster-mother immediately adopts her calf or calves. And there are many recorded cases of courageous actions by elephants in aid of a wounded comrade. When a member of a herd is shot or otherwise hurt, and falls to the ground, two or three others will stay with it whilst the rest hasten away to safety, thrusting their trunks beneath its huge body, and making every effort to help it to its feet again so that it can rejoin the group. If it is helpless, or dead, they will sometimes stand beside it for hours before abandoning it.

Yet perhaps the most pleasingly affectionate of all family relationships in the wilds is that uniting a group of the supposedly most ferocious of all beasts—lions. I remember a pride at Amboseli consisting of the male who was its lord and master, three lionesses among whom he distributed his favours, and two litters of cubs which were the results of those favours towards a couple of the females—one litter containing six-week-old triplets, and the other a pair of three-day-old twins. We first came upon them feasting on a dead giraffe lying already largely disembowelled on the ground. The lion—who always claims the prerogative of taking first cuts at the meat—had eaten his fill, and was lying snoozing contentedly close by whilst the rest of the family were taking their turn at the banquet. The three lionesses were licking and tearing at various parts of the giraffe whilst the six-week-old cubs merely played at licking and tearing at it. No doubt the youngsters were enjoying some of their first tastes of blood; but their efforts were otherwise make-believe rehearsals for later serious meals, since they were still too tiny for the substantial consumption of anything more than their mothers' milk. The litter of three-day-old cubs was not on view. A game-scout with us explained that they stayed concealed among near-by bushes because their eyes had not yet opened, and they were still too feeble for coherent movement on four legs.

Every now and then the youngsters at the kill got bored with the lifeless corpse, and crawled away to their dozing father, hoping to stir him into more entertaining life. They would playfully bite his tail or paw at his body—impertinent disturbances of his siesta which he usually accepted in the comradely spirit in which they were offered. Raising his head, he would look out of the corners of his eyes at his mischievous offspring, partly in protest but mostly with paternal tolerance. But at the same time he flicked his tail or stretched a leg in mild warning that their liberties should not be pushed too far. And occasionally when a cub persisted beyond the adult's view of what was reasonable, he would

33

'a mother lioness'

give it a light cuff on an ear, in which parental discipline was judiciously tempered by fatherly affection. Then he would lie down and continue his snooze, whilst the youngsters scampered back to their mother and 'aunts' in the hope of finding them more interested in a game.

One of the most attractive elements in lion family life is the relationship between a mother lioness, her own cubs, their aunts, and those aunts' cubs. We watched an example of it late the following afternoon when we returned for another glimpse of the pride. One lioness was sitting near a path with the three older cubs gambolling round her. Half-a-mile away across the wide plain we could see the lion and the so far cubless lioness dallying together. From their behaviour it was evident that he was courting her, and that they were temporarily detached from the rest of the group on one of those honeymoons which are characteristic of lions' domestic life, and which I shall describe later in this book.

The third lioness was nowhere in sight. Our expert game-scout told us that she had gone hunting on the previous evening, and that she had evidently made no quick kill, since she was still away. He furthermore informed us that the absent huntress was the mother of the six-week-old trio of youngsters, and that she had left them in the meantime in the charge of the aunt with whom we now watched them. That was the normal procedure between lionesses in the same pride, who have a most sisterly relationship of mutual confidence, and who regularly act as baby-sitters for each other. This aunt was in fact the mother of the pair of few-days-old cubs still hidden in the near-by bushes. No doubt she kept a sharp look-out against any possible danger to her own babies whilst she did her duty towards her nephews and nieces.

She sat relaxed but watchful as those latter youngsters played around her. Their antics were very kitten-like, which was not surprising since lions are the pre-eminent members of

34

'cuffing each other gently'

the cat tribe. They rolled over the ground together in mock wrestling matches, cuffing each other gently, biting each others' tails, and grabbing stalks of grass in their teeth to use in games of tug-of-war. Then they started playing catch-as-catch-can with their auntie's tail, pouncing on its hairy tip, nibbling at its sleek length, and poking it this way and that. She flicked it gently to and fro, joining in the game. Afterwards they nuzzled at her legs, climbed over her body, and patted her face with their paws. With the utmost tenderness she responded by licking them; and then she lay down at full stretch to enable them to clamber all over her. When they tired of that sport they jumped off her, and resumed their tomfoolery among themselves. Neither she nor they showed any concern whatever at our land-rover standing a few yards away, with Chris's camera clicking occasional photographs.

Every now and then the cubs stopped their lively activities and stared towards the horizon, always in the same direction. Our game-scout explained that their mother must have departed into that region when she left on the previous evening, and that they were watching for her return. When he made a clever imitation of a lioness's soft call out of our car window, they pricked up their ears and ran towards us, looking around hopefully. The scout said they must be hungry, as they had not fed for twenty-four hours.

Towards dusk a lioness's call—exactly like his imitations—sounded from another direction. Looking there, we saw the mother returning with leisurely, dignified steps, seeming rather tired. The cubs, too, caught sight of her, and for a while they stood staring at her sceptically, as if this could not possibly be her returning from that unexpected quarter of the compass. Then she called again, and at once the tiny trio romped to her, pawed at her fondly, and trotted along excitedly at her feet as she continued to stroll to their home base.

35

The aunt stayed lying in the grass, watching with satisfaction the reunion of the mother and children, content that her spell of duty as nursemaid was once more over. The returning huntress halted near her, and then lay down as if exhausted. At once the three cubs snuggled to the row of nipples protruding along her chest and belly, beginning to suck them. I noticed that they propped their fore-paws against her body, and occasionally pressed them against it so as to aid the flow of milk. Later the lioness rose and walked deliberately across to the aunt, and nuzzled and licked her in a display of affection, as if to say, 'Thank you, my dear, for looking after the kids so well.'

All that time the lion and his new lady-love stayed side by side at a distance across the plain, absorbed in each other's company, forgetful for the time being of the other members of their pride.

X

But I must not become sentimental about such episodes. They represent the charmingly gentle, even loving side of wild life—and they have their counterpart in a crueller side. The massacre of a myriad creatures by countless others goes on all the time. A bird-watcher observes it whenever he sees the parents of numerous species feed their chicks in a nest. Even the most innocent-looking, exquisitely fairy-like creatures like little sunbirds are unmitigated murderers. Minute after minute, hour after hour, and day after day in the breeding seasons they bring a succession of slaughtered insects to nourish their growing nestlings, just as for that same inexorable purpose eagles kill hares, herons catch fish, storks slay frogs, hornbills grab beetles, starlings seize caterpillars, and all manner of other carnivorous and insectivorous birds destroy all sorts of other prey.

The same is true of every kind of predator on land, water and air. The killings do not always seem so inoffensive as when a robin carries an ugly worm to its brood of charming fledglings. The spectacle of a pack of African wild dogs giving merciless chase to a pretty gazelle, and then tearing it to bits alive, is not attractive; and the same can be said of a hyena gorging on an antelope fawn, a leopard pouncing on a cheeky little monkey, or a pride of lions violently despatching a zebra. But they are all similar innocent acts of obedience to the law of Nature. They play their parts in achieving the preservation of every species, maintaining the survival of the fittest of each kind, and so promoting a vigorous, healthy balance of existence among the infinite, grand variety of creatures which inhabit the Earth.

XI

Animal, and especially bird, photography is not an easy, comfortable pastime. If it sometimes secures triumphant results, they are often preceded by severe trials and tribulations.

36

A typical example of that sequence of events occurred when we sought to get pictures of a pair of secretary birds and their chick at a nest. Apparently no one had hitherto succeeded in taking really good colour shots of those imposing creatures at home; and so when Bill Langridge found a nest twenty-three miles from Larry Wateridge's house in the Mara Reserve, Larry invited us all to go and stay with him there, and we packed our cameras, field-glasses, flashlamps and other paraphernalia, and set out.

The season was mid-April, and the long rains had commenced. They reached a climax on the evening of our arrival at Larry's bungalow. Throughout that night a torrential downpour descended from the heavens upon the earth. However, the next morning dawned fair; and soon after sunrise Chris, Bill, Larry, some African assistants and I set forth hopefully in a land-rover. It took us three hours to cover the first nineteen miles across rough, rain-sodden country; but our spirits soared when we managed to ford two flooded streams which our guides informed us would be the most serious obstacles in our path. Then, four miles short of our goal, we reached a five-foot-deep stream of rushing water which (they declared) had not flowed even an inch deep when they made a reconnaissance trip on the previous day. It had suddenly appeared from nowhere! Yet it was anything but a mirage. During that mockingly sunny morning and afternoon we returned to the spot several times in the expectation that the torrent would have subsided, and that we could cross it. But it maintained its forbidding depth, and we could never drive our vehicle through it. Apparently it was being steadily reinforced by natural drainage from some neighbouring hills; so in the evening we retraced our nineteen miles bumpy journey home in a frustrated mood.

That night more rain fell; but the next morning broke fair once more; and we repeated our attempt, having despatched a work-party well ahead of us to build a tree-trunk foot-bridge across the torrent. We had also sent a second land-rover to make a long detour and await us on the water's further shore. Sure enough, the rather precarious bridge held firm, and in half-an-hour we transported all the precious cameras, flashlamps, tripods, picnic baskets, bottles of drink, and ourselves from the first land-rover into the second. At the end of a further four miles uneventful drive we arrived on the stroke of twelve noon safe, sound and expectant at the secretary birds' nest. The mother bird was strolling across the ground below a thorn tree, having evidently just fed her solitary youngster in their nest on the tree's flat top.

The weather was promisingly dry, with periodic spells of sunshine. After carrying the photographic equipment up a twenty-foot ladder into the hide, clipping obstructive foliage from around the nest, and installing Chris on her hidden platform, the rest of us withdrew to observe events from a discreet half-mile away. Five minutes later rain began to fall; within ten minutes it had gathered forbidding force; and for the next five hours it continued its drenching descent with only brief intervals of respite. Neither parent bird visited the nest, probably because their hunting was fruitless in the downpour. Nor did the half-grown nestling offer Chris more than one fleeting opportunity to take a good portrait, for it lay low all the rest of the time in evident discomfort. Once it did stand up to stretch its legs, and she immediately snapped a shot of it; but it promptly retorted by flopping down into a low, suspicious crouch. After that it never stirred again.

Towards dusk we rescued Chris from the hide—wet, chilled and sneezing, but with serene patience unruffled by her long, uncomfortable vigil because for some unaccountable reason she felt optimistic about the prospect of the morrow.

No rain fell that night; soon after sunrise the next day our land-rover crossed all the rivulets without difficulty; and by mid-morning Chris and her photographic equipment were settled once more in the hide. As she climbed into its tent, and the rest of us withdrew, I noticed both adult secretary birds strutting among bushes fifty yards away, evidently well stocked with food, and waiting for our departure before going to feed their youngster. Bill, a guide and I took up position for observations at our usual spot half-a-mile away— and five minutes later we saw the mother bird alight on the nest.

She stayed there several minutes before flying off again. About an hour later the cock bird came to the nest edge; but he remained only a few seconds, and then took wing without delivering food to the nestling, apparently frightened by the camera's click as Chris took a picture of him. After about another hour the hen returned once more, and a minute later the father bird alighted beside her on the nest. But again he flew off a few moments afterwards when Chris took a photograph of the family group. The hen remained several minutes longer, her maternal instinct overcoming any concern she may have felt at the sounds of the camera taking shot after shot of her and her offspring.

The sun continued to shine obligingly; but neither parent returned during the next three hours, presumably indulging in the siesta which many animals observe through the hottest part of the day. At three-thirty Bill expressed apprehension to me about an electric storm which he claimed to see gathering on the horizon, and which he declared would come flying straight in our direction. He feared that since Chris's hide stood on the highest spot of ground in the vicinity, its meccano-like metal Dexion framework might attract the impending lightning, with fatal results for the photographic equipment, if not for the photographer herself. He urged that we should go and fetch her away from exposure to that risk. So we went and called her down to earth. I did it reluctantly, and with a private feeling of criticism of Bill for being unduly cautious—for the sky seemed to me to be reasonably clear, and I felt that if we had left Chris aloft for another half-hour the secretary birds would have returned to commence their next bout of feeding, and she would have got another set of pictures of them.

But how right Bill was! He always judged with expert accuracy the moods of the African skies. A dark cloud flew swiftly towards us, and no sooner had we packed Chris and her belongings safely into the land-rover than raindrops began to fall. Within a few minutes the storm broke with a vengeance. The sky became black, lightning seared the murky heavens, thunder roared, and rain descended in thick sheets, clattering all over our vehicle like a mob of hailstones running amok.

We made every possible speed homewards, our land-rover plunging through a drenching atmosphere. Soon the well-worn, rutted track beneath the car's wheels lay submerged several inches in running water, and every few moments our view through the windscreen became completely obscured by torrential rain pouring down from above and by liquid mud leaping up from the tyres below. But the windscreen-wipers worked gallantly, making it possible most of the time for the driver to see a sufficient few yards ahead to keep us on the right path. He urged the car forward as rapidly as the inclement conditions would permit, for it was important that we should ford the series of rivulets ahead before they became impassably swollen. So the land-rover bumped, skidded and jumped over the rough ground as we forged erratically ahead. At one moment a flash of lightning struck a tree twenty yards behind us, splitting its trunk with a loud crack which momentarily silenced all the tempest's other roars. By good luck and firm, courageous driving, we reached the streams in time, and just managed to cross them without mishap. Their depths were rising quickly; and if we had been a few minutes slower we would have been too late, and would have got marooned out-of-doors in the infuriated elements.

The downpour continued, and as we progressed across the plain it seemed more as if we sat in a submarine ploughing through a wild sea than in a motor car crossing 'dry land'. I would not have been surprised to observe fish swimming past our rain-washed windows, and would have thought it natural if a family of diving hippopotamuses had suddenly appeared there. Instead we caught occasional shadowy views through veils of water of herds of gazelles sitting unperturbed by their drenching.

Nature's moods are incalculable. When we arrived within a few miles of Larry's house the storm ceased as suddenly as it had started. The elements having demonstrated forcibly to us that it lay in their power to destroy all our efforts (if not also us ourselves) at any moment they chose, they perhaps relented and decided to grant us a glimpse of the bene-volent side of their temperaments too. The rain-clouds raced away elsewhere, and soon afterwards a coy sun appeared in the sky. Nor was that Nature's only concession, for a moment later we caught sight of a beautiful cheetah sitting beside our track, gazing in our direction almost as if it were expecting us, and posing as if its sole purpose in life were to become a model for Christina Loke's camera.

However, when we slowed our pace and advanced cautiously towards it in the hope of satisfying that apparent whim, the beast rose and bounded away in contrary temper. Yet after a while it stopped, and threw a glance back at us, almost as if to say, 'Come along, there's a better setting for photography over here.' We discreetly continued our pursuit; and the handsome great cat waited for a minute. Then as we drew almost near enough for a snapshot it moved away again, betraying still a certain suspicious resentment at our trailing it. We stopped, and it too immediately slackened speed, strolled a few more steps with nonchalant, athletic grace, and then halted. We started to follow once more, but hesitated for a while at a prudent distance away to take preliminary shots of it, in case we got no better chances. Then we moved nearer. It rose and walked onwards, but this time at an easy, leisurely pace, seeming reassured and only mildly curious at the approach of the four-wheeled monster inside whose belly we sat. No doubt it assumed the car to be some fellow inhabitant of the wild, perhaps a strange metallic, engine-purring member of the cat family. And gradually, in the course of a succession of mutually cautious but tolerant progressions and halts by both parties during the next half hour, the lovely beast lost all concern at us, accepted completely our harmless companionship, and allowed us to come ever closer during its periods of rest. Sometimes it rose and sauntered slowly away from us, sometimes it hesitated and gazed contemplatively in our direction, sometimes it stood and stared at different objects in the landscape, and at other times it squatted relaxedly on its haunches before us, or lay down and acted for us as if it were a tame cheetah performing in a film studio. So Chris got a remarkable series of pictures of it.

When dusk fell we left it, and turned homewards once more.

Larry had stayed indoors that day, to do a lot of his Tsetse Control Officer's chores urgently demanding his attention. As we arrived before his door he stepped on to the verandah, and held up a warning finger at us.

'I'm afraid,' he said, 'a new guest has arrived to stay in the house. He's another V.I.P., and he's in the sitting-room looking forward to meeting you. If I may, I'll introduce you as soon as we go in.'

I felt annoyed. I was convalescing after pneumonia, and was under strict doctor's orders to do no work whatever, to avoid all official contacts, to see no one on business, and to rest completely. I was obeying those instructions with enthusiasm, and enjoying complete relaxation with my naturalist friends. The last wild creature I wished to meet in the Mara Game Reserve was a strange V.I.P. who would no doubt be eager to talk endlessly about the latest political situations in Kenya, Africa and the world.

But it was too late to escape; and I could think of no plausible excuse to retire and sulk in my bedroom for the rest of the evening.

We entered the sitting-room. A smiling African servant waited to receive our orders for drinks before dinner. I looked around the place expectantly, apprehensively; but no one else was in view.

'The new house-guest is there,' said Larry, pointing to a large wooden box on the floor in a corner of the room.

We went to it, and saw a small lion cub curled up asleep like a puppy on a bed of freshly plucked grasses.

Larry told us that one of his assistants had heard strange, baby-like whimpers coming from a patch of undergrowth near the house soon after the day's awful storm had passed. Going to the spot, he spied the little creature half sunk in the ground, solitary, wet, muddy, and whining miserably. Not more than two weeks old, it had somehow got separated from its mother in the tempest.

Larry explained that when lionesses are caring for very young cubs they change the lairs in which they lodge them every two or three days. That is presumably an instinctive precaution against observation and murder by watchful hyenas or other enemies of helpless infants. Possibly this youngster's mother was moving house when the storm suddenly broke, and in the howling gale she accidentally lost touch with it. Or perhaps it took fright, crawled astray from some customary hiding place, and never re-established contact with

40

'a small lion cub curled up asleep'

its parent. She may have had one or two other cubs to look after, and not have dared to leave them to go in search of the missing waif.

The tiny lion now looked hale if not hearty in its soap-box; but occasionally it emitted a small, heartrending whimper or growl, obviously calling for its mother. Larry thought its chances of survival at such a delicate age under exotic human care were dubious, although so far it was responding to friendly treatment with an encouraging degree of reluctant acceptance. For example, after several vain attempts to coax it that afternoon, it had eventually fallen to the temptation to appease its hunger by swallowing a spoonful of milk, a sip of Farex and Lactogen baby food, and a tot of Hennessy's Three Star brandy. To help it in its struggle to live through the next few critical days Larry had already telephoned to Nairobi for the speediest possible delivery in Mara of supplies of cod-liver oil, calcium (to help the healthy formation of its bones and teeth), and other specialised nourishment.

By the next day the little orphan was sucking willingly for a while every hour at the rubber teat of a human baby's bottle filled with slightly warmed cow's milk. Whilst it drank it squatted on its hind-legs and waved its two fore-paws pushfully at the empty air in front of it, performing instinctively the action which I had already observed in the case of the young lions being suckled by their mother at Amboseli, when they kept pressing their paws against her stomach to aid the steady flow of milk through her teats.

The cub looked like a soft little puppy, though with a slightly gruffer face than most

41

puppies wear. Its senses of sight and hearing were not yet strongly developed, and it seemed at a loss in its new environment. Much of the time it spent asleep, curled up on its side with its head clutched between its fore-paws, or stretched on its back with all its legs pointing up into space. Whenever it woke it made quite loud gruntings or sort of barkings, presumably informing its mother of its whereabouts. Sometimes it uttered them in its sleep, as if it were dreaming nostalgically of its proper existence. Then it would stagger up, and crawl slowly over the floor, partly on its legs and partly on its stomach, unsteadily and searchingly, as if it could not quite remember what it was looking for.

It turned out to be a female, and in remembrance of my association with her discovery Larry christened her Flora MacDonald. Later she lived for some time in the wild beasts' orphanage in the Nairobi National Park, where the authorities gave her the official name of Mara to denote her place of origin. She has survived triumphantly, and as I write this note she is a healthy and particularly beautiful eighteen-month-old lioness who is about to start on a career as a film actress. I went to visit her the other day at Naro Moru, where she and a small group of other lions are encamped on astonishingly friendly terms with Virginia McKenna, Bill Travers and the other actors, producers and photographers engaged in making the film *Born Free*.

XII

Fortunately the movement of world opinion, including all-important African opinion, in favour of preserving Africa's wild life is gaining ground. The wise and great Mzee Jomo Kenyatta and his Government in Kenya are in the vanguard of those striving for the cause. They feel proud of their country's natural heritage, and recognise that it can add distinctly to Kenya's fame and fortune. The authorities in Tanzania and Uganda think likewise.

There are many practical as well as sentimental reasons for maintaining East Africa's multitudes of game animals. For example, much African country is not really suitable for agricultural cultivation, owing to the quality of the soil; and the planting of crops in those regions would be counter-productive. Nor is cattle and sheep ranching always the right answer in such places, because on certain types of land wild beasts are more economical feeders than domestic animals would be. The latter overgraze the local vegetation, render the earth impotent, and so destroy the area's fruitfulness, causing it before long to become semi-desert. For some reason various game animals are more discreet feeders and fertilisers, and such territory should therefore be reserved for the types of these which have lived there for centuries. Other considerable regions can successfully sustain domestic cattle, sheep and goats, but only within certain limits; and the most productive use of such areas could often be made by a judicious combination of herds of domestic animals with herds of wild beasts sharing their pasturage. Yet other areas can best be used for either pure ranching or crop cultivation.

There is another significant consideration. Across much of East Africa's grazing and browsing regions game animals yield a larger quantity of better meat per acre than would be the case if it were occupied by even the finest breeds of beef and mutton flesh. That is true with reference to types like elephants, buffaloes and various antelopes which can provide the good protein-rich food which many African peoples at present lack. It is wiser therefore to reserve certain regions for cropping those beasts than it would be to hand them over for raising cattle or sheep. So one can 'kill two birds with one stone'—provide needed meat for Africa's human population, and preserve species of wild animals which might otherwise become extinct.

This is not the place to write in more detail of those problems. Various related questions arise, such as that of the maintenance of adequate forests. A comprehensive expert survey of East African (as well as other African) land should be made, to decide which regions can best be devoted wholly to agriculture or husbandry, which should support judicious mixtures of both wild beasts and domestic cattle, sheep or goats, and which should be entirely protected as nature reserves.

It will not always be easy to persuade some of the African tribes concerned that such policies are wise. For example, the Masai own more than 15,000 square miles of Kenya alone, as well as an immense area in neighbouring Tanzania; and so their agreement must be secured to any plans touching the use of those lands. They are pastoralists; for them the measure of a man's wealth is the number of his cattle; and they are inclined to love and prize their bulls and cows more dearly than life itself. Their instinct is therefore to expand their domestic herds indefinitely, regardless of any other consideration. Traditionally they themselves eat little meat, since they are drinkers of cow's milk and blood, with some vegetarian diet thrown in for good measure, and just an occasional sliver of beef. So they are not hunters of game, and are uninterested in preserving wild beasts as prospective supplies of food. For them such animals are merely potential rivals for the grazing lands of their precious expanding herds of cattle. It is therefore difficult to arouse their enthusiasm for the cause of the preservation of wild life. They cannot easily understand why zebras, wildebeests, antelopes and other competitors for their cows' pastures should be treated with respect, and still less why lions, leopards and similar likely murderers of those cattle should be especially protected.

These proud, handsome, very likeable people live in small, circular, thorn-hedged *manyattas* or villages scattered all over Masailand. Their young men are now denied the first of their three main traditional occupations—waging war—and so they concentrate on the other two, herding cattle and courting. And of the three, the greatest has always been herding cattle.

Similar peoples with similar ways of life inhabit other considerable areas of Kenya's wilds. All round Maralal, for example, the Samburu are the local landlords. They too are nomadic pastoralists with large, wandering herds of cattle. When they are not busy tending their beasts they often engage in singing, dancing and feasting. I shall never forget a day at Maralal when I was studiously watching large parties of pelicans, ibises,

43

'small, circular, thorn-hedged manyattas or villages'

geese, ducks and other water-fowl disporting on a small lake. The time was early afternoon; the hot mid-day sunshine was almost oppressively intense, and a siesta hush lay upon Nature all around. I thought I was the only human being in the spacious, untamed, tranquil landscape; and I was very content with my solitude.

Suddenly the silence was broken by a burst of some of the most beautiful human singing that I have ever heard. Looking into the skies and across the earth to discern its origin, I saw that it came from a thorn-hedged, hut-filled manyatta on a hilltop about half-a-mile away, where Samburu villagers were evidently celebrating a wedding. I laid down my field-glasses, leaned against a tree, forgot about all other Nature, and for the next hour enjoyed a most pleasing concert.

The preservation of Kenya's treasure of wild life depends largely on gaining the cooperation of such peoples as the Masai, the Samburu, the Turkana, the Meru, and other similar tribes who own vast areas of the country involved. If they permit their flocks and herds of cattle and goats to grow too large, to compete unduly with the other beasts in cropping the vegetation, and to impoverish the soil by over-grazing and over-browsing, the wild life will disappear and die. Attendant on such competition is also an inevitable warfare—predators attacking the cattle, and the cattle-owners shooting the predators— which quickens the pace at which certain species will become extinct. The danger is of

44

course aggravated where the local people are poachers for elephant ivory, rhinoceros horn, leopard skins, and other prized trophies.

Therefore part of the problem of wild-life preservation consists in finding ways of persuading these tribesmen that if they destroy the game, they are depriving themselves of an asset which can be of great value to them. They are not altruists who will agree to protect lions, elephants, zebras, and other animals useless to them for the beasts' own dear sakes; nor are they yet scientists, aesthetes or sentimentalists who will cherish them for zoological or artistic reasons. They are typically self-centred, earthy human beings; and if their aid is to be enlisted they must be shown that they themselves will receive material gain from solicitous consideration for four-footed wild creatures. If that is proved to them, their shrewd good sense will make a helpful response.

Happily this sort of education is now taking place. They are beginning to understand— what few people ever seriously tried to teach them before—that if they will withdraw their cattle altogether from certain areas, and cease hunting and poaching there, and allow great herds of antelopes, prides of lions, troops of giraffes, families of ostriches, and multitudes of other beasts to thrive, then herds of other odd creatures called tourists will also flock to those places, to enjoy the sights of spacious natural zoological gardens. And the tourists will bring money, and spend it there, and leave it behind them when they depart.

The Masai at Mara, the Samburu at Uaso Nyiro, the Meru beside Mount Kenya, and other tribes elsewhere are now consenting to withdraw their cattle at least tentatively from considerable tracts of their land, so that those areas can become protected wild animal reserves—and so that they themselves can receive as annual rent a goodly percentage of the profits made from tourists. Nor are they ready to do that solely for the reason of material gain. Their wisest leaders tell them also that the animals are a treasure belonging not to Kenya alone, but to the whole world; and they begin to comprehend that this adds to the prestige of their homeland. It fosters their awakening pride in the new, young Kenyan nation.

XIII

This book makes no claim to being an authoritative work on animals inhabiting Kenya. Even if I possessed the qualifications to write such a volume—which I do not—I have been kept so almost constantly busy with other compelling concerns during these historic times in East Africa that I have enjoyed little leisure to devote to my neighbours in Nairobi's National Park, and to their relatives elsewhere. Incidentally, that may make the book more intriguing for other ordinary people like myself in Europe, America, Asia or the Antipodes who have a liking for wild animals, but no particular knowledge of them, and who are attracted by the idea of visiting Africa to view them; because these pages demonstrate in a casual, inexpert way exactly the experiences which any tourists can encounter during such an expedition.

The book describes only a tiny selection of the attractive birds and beasts who will greet such visitors, and it is not arranged here according to any learned zoological protocol or scientific table of precedence. The animals are mixed up higgledy-piggledy together. In fact they make their appearances page after page much as the living creatures might present themselves, one after another, within view of a party of trippers in any of Kenya's game sanctuaries. Their order of entry would not be exactly the same, because as a matter of convenience in this volume they have been arranged in alphabetical sequence according to their common-or-garden English names—and, of course, none of these animals has yet learned the ABC.

What does give this volume very fine distinction is its brilliant gallery of photographs by Christina Loke. Having been hailed by authorities as 'the finest bird photographer in Asia', she now takes her place as one of the pre-eminent portrayers of Africa's birds and beasts. It is a great pleasure to write notes for the noble pageant of her pictures which parade across the pages of this book.

The Plates

Avocet

Recurvirostra avosetta

East Africa is wonderfully rich in every type of animal life, from the largest beasts to the smallest insects. Its multitudinous variety of fish is a typical example. In the Eastern African countries more than 1,000 species of fresh-water fish are to be found, compared with about sixty in the whole of Europe. Again 1,035 different species of birds have been recorded in Kenya alone, and more than 1,400 in Kenya, Uganda and Tanzania, compared with 577 throughout Europe, including Britain but excluding Russia. As for such small fry as butterflies, moths, beetles and other insects, their teeming legions are unnumbered.

A great majority of Kenya's birds are residents, whilst others come as seasonal migrants from Europe or Asia, as well as from other parts of Africa. Among them none is more graceful than the avocet. Members of the species are mostly winter visitors to Africa, where they arrive in very large quantities towards the year's end. Their favourite haunts in East Africa then are the various lakes spilt along the Great Rift Valley; and sometimes they gather on them in huge flocks containing thousands and even tens of thousands of birds. A competent observer in November 1940 reported a multitude of between 10,000 and 30,000 avocets assembled on Lake Manyara in Tanzania—which must have been a massively pretty sight.

The bird has an elegant figure, with a sharply contrasting snow-white and pitch-black body poised on top of tall blue-grey legs, and with a long, thin, upward-turning beak extending from its graceful head. As it wades through shallow waters in search of prey it picks up its webbed feet carefully; and in deeper water it shows itself a buoyant swimmer. Its diet is shrimps and darting aquatic insects, which it scoops in by scythe-like sweeps of its bill from side to side as it marches or swims forwards. The photograph of a bird so engaged on the opposite page has not the same brilliant quality as many other pictures in this book; but we decided to include it because the avocet adds such a unique touch of grace to Kenya's wild menagerie.

A comparatively small number of the species stays to mate in East Africa. Many instances of their breeding on Kenya's lakes and marshes have been recorded, one of their regular nesting sites being Lake Magadi. They lay their eggs in slight scoops on dried mud or sand, sometimes among short grasses, and usually in colonies. Their newborn chicks are as pretty as any fluffy youngsters could be.

Baboon

Papio anubis

No anthropoid apes live in Kenya. Chimpanzees and gorillas are neighbours in Tanzania and Uganda; but in Kenya the biggest similar creature—apart from Man himself—is the baboon.

Large groups of these engaging animals move across the wild countryside, usually within sprinting distance of trees in regions frequented by leopards, which are their only serious enemies. Their communal life is full of noisy charm, and is governed by a patriarchal hierarchy. The old males exert a strong authority, compelling strict obedience from their juniors. Mothers and their youngsters are inseparable. Whilst a nursing mother squats on her bare-skinned posterior munching food, her baby clings with both arms and legs round her body, sucking or snoozing. When she rises and strolls on all fours across the ground it tightens its hold, and hangs beneath her stomach like a bomb slung beneath an aeroplane; or occasionally it sprawls on her back like a helpless rider on a runaway horse. When it grows older, however, it sits upright there like a jockey as she saunters along, with its hands held free to pluck and nibble passing bits of grass, or to scratch itself nonchalantly as its old-man's eyes survey the surrounding scene. Sometimes when alarmed the elder breaks into a gallop; and I have seen her then seize the youngster in her mouth by the scruff of its neck, and grip it as it swings violently but docilely from side to side.

Adult males often approach a female and stretch out an arm to be de-bugged; and in return they perform a similar service for her. Such grooming is an act of friendship, and sometimes of courtship; and as a result of it baboons are among the cleanliest of all wild animals. I once watched a matron sitting with a look of utter boredom on her face whilst her small baby clung to her breast sucking at her nipples, and a big male explored with searching fingers every inch of her body. He may or may not have been the infant's father, since baboons of both sexes are promiscuous. He enjoyed good hunting, frequently discovering a parasite or a mite of loose salty skin lodged behind her ears, beneath an armpit, between her thighs, or in some other nook or cranny of her anatomy. Promptly he plucked it off with his eager fingers or teeth. Periodically his examination brought him to the vicinity of the youngster's feeding, and his hands began to fumble at the maternal bosom. Reluctantly the babe would loose its lip-hold on her teats, and wait patiently but frustratedly until he had finished his local explorations. Then it resumed sucking. Once its patience wore thin before he completed a bout of meticulous searchings; and it sought to recommence feeding too soon. He became annoyed, and gave the brat a cuff with a severe parental or avuncular paw. It was an example of the stern discipline, as well as fond affection, with which elders in wild animal society bring up their youngsters.

Troops of baboons spend most of the day patrolling wide areas of ground for food, only resorting to trees to sleep at nights—except when they scamper up them to escape a

leopard's attentions. Often they also use high ledges on steep rock faces as dormitories, where their genius for climbing makes them equally at home, and where they are safer from sudden attack by their cunning foe. Wherever they travel they normally walk on all fours, only occasionally standing erect on hind-legs to scrutinise some distant view in case of possible danger lurking there. Baboons' eyes, deep-set beneath beetling brows, have one of the keenest sights in the animal world, their power of vision being reckoned equal to that of a man using a powerful pair of binoculars.

They eat roots, wild fruits, eggs, grubs, spiders and other insects, including even scorpions—being careful when they catch that last delicacy to deprive it first of its sting-laden tail. They possess long, sharp teeth which make them dangerous antagonists. Although they usually take to flight at any glimpse of a leopard—chattering and screaming their displeasure as they go—they do not lack courage when a situation demands it; and they will attack the enemy if it fumbles an assault on a member of their troop. In such circumstances leopards have been torn to pieces by the formidable teeth of an enraged mob of baboons.

In other situations their conduct is more amusing to watch. When a party is idling between meals its members often engage in games like a crowd of lively and mischievous human children. The authority of the masculine gang bosses then becomes evident, for they discipline with scolds and smacks any youngsters whose pranks exceed recognised baboonish proprieties. Sometimes a baboon leaps on the back of an impala to enjoy a ride, an impertinence at which the mount usually shows mild surprise, but no resentment. And often the skittish animals jump on the bonnets of tourists' cars in the National Parks, to beg for food with outstretched hands at the windows. Too much encouragement then can produce a risky state of affairs. If, for example, a baboon thinks that a stroke or other gesture by a child is intended in hostility, it can launch an immediate attack with grabbing paws and ferocious teeth. Adult males in particular are moody and unpredictable in temper, especially when they feel thwarted or threatened. It is prudent to take no risks with them.

The engaging mother and child with a boy friend on the previous page belong to the species called Olive Baboon, as does the husky fellow crossing a stream opposite.

False Vampire Bat

Cardioderma cor

Among the seventy-three species of bats so far recorded in Kenya two belong to the Family Megadermidae, or False Vampire (or Big-eared) Bats. They are so called because of an imagined resemblance to the true vampires. The specimen shown opposite is a Heart-nosed False Vampire, which normally inhabits caves, but which in this instance chose to share Larry Wateridge's sitting-room with him and his guests. There it hung upside-down beneath the ceiling all day long every day.

The species is remarkable because in addition to its usual insect food it sometimes consumes other, smaller types of bats, and perhaps also even little rodents. John Williams, whose enthusiasm for studying winged creatures extends very learnedly from birds to bats, has found evidence of that in the form of remnants of meals eaten in caverns frequented by this type of false vampire. However, further researches on the subject are required because so far no one has ever seen it actually catching its prey.

The method by which bats capture their victims is an intriguing subject. Since their eyes are not adapted for seeing by night (as are those of owls and cats) some other sense is involved. Careful observations and experiments reveal it to be the phenomenon of echo-location: by emitting ultrasonic sound-pulses bats not only find their way, but also locate their prey, in the dark. This radar equipment then guides them to their targets. Naturally the threatened moths have evolved their own devices for counter-detection; and in the cases of many species this is believed to take the form of sensitive 'ultrasonic ears' situated in a pocket on each side of their bodies, which enable those would-be victims to discern the presence of their enemies, and to take evasive action. If that is a correct deduction, a sort of constant wireless warfare must be waged between bats and moths throughout the nights. When a bat wins a contest it gathers its victim by a scoop with a wing, and conveys the prize to its mouth.

Unfortunately Mankind has not yet invented any similar method of guidance to the whereabouts of bats; and so these creatures remain among the least known of East African mammals. The numerous cave-dwelling species are fairly well recorded, for they are easier to find than others which sleep amidst the foliage, below the bark, beneath the mosses, or in holes up the trunks of forest trees. Many specimens have probably therefore been overlooked hitherto; but they are now being increasingly discovered. The list of Kenya's resident species is likely to grow considerably in the coming years.

Cinnamon-chested Bee-eater

Melittophagus oreobates

The bee-eater shown opposite is flying into its nest in an earth-bank just outside a busy kitchen window at Mara. The pair of birds betrayed little or no concern at the comings and goings of the human inhabitants of the house, and of domestic cocks and hens, motor cars, a pet lion, and other creatures constantly around. April was drawing towards its close, and the bee-eaters were incubating eggs. Their clutch was hidden at the far end of a narrow, foot-long tunnel excavated by the birds themselves.

Both sexes of Cinnamon-chested Bee-eaters wear the same beautiful plumage; so I could not tell whether the hen or the cock did most of the incubating. On the first day of my observations my impression was that the female spent nearly all her time on the nest whilst her mate brought food to her there, for I saw one bird carry captured insects several times to the other concealed indoors. Just occasionally the sitter emerged outside the nest, presumably to stretch its wings for a while; and the forager then gave it food whilst it perched on a nearby bough.

On a later day when I watched them both birds shared more or less equally the tedious labour of incubation, each relieving the other on the nest at intervals ranging from forty minutes to about an hour. Neither bee-eater brought food to the other then, each doing its own hunting during its spells off duty. Possibly on the previous occasion the hen had just completed laying her set of eggs, and maternal instinct demanded that she should be for a while their sole guardian.

The bird outside the nest rarely strayed far away. Almost always it perched on a tree a dozen yards from the tunnel in the earth-bank. Probably it was performing a sentinel function there, since the bee-eater inside the nest could not keep a look-out for possible approaching enemies. However, that guardian cinnamon-breasted angel was at the same time very occupied with feeding itself. It scarcely ever remained stationary on a twig for more than a few seconds before it leaped into the air again in pursuit of some fresh passing flying-insect. Its swiftly darting, swooping, swerving, soaring and diving movements as it chased its victim through the air were a demonstration of exquisitely beautiful, masterful flight. Only when it engaged in a bout of preening its feathers—and when it returned to the nest for a spell of incubation duty—did it permit itself a little rest. Nevertheless, it was no doubt always alertly and protectively conscious of its home a few yards away, and of its mate sitting on their progeny within.

Dung Beetle

Scarabaeus sacer

Many millions of beetles belonging to more than 20,000 different species in this wide-spread family crawl across Africa, Southern Europe and Asia. Most of them subsist on animals' dung, which they fashion into a ball, and then roll into a hiding-place for later consumption. Not every species treats the tasty muck in precisely that manner; but many of them do, and it was the customary method of the little creatures in Tsavo Park shown on the opposite page.

One beetle alone was the actual creator of the dung-ball. When that industrious animal's handiwork was complete it started to convey the stuff to a suitable spot for burial. Since the sphere was too large to be picked up and carried, the beetle turned its back on the ball, did a 'hand-stand' on its front feet, propped its hind-legs against the dung's surface, and then began to run backwards, trundling the ball ahead of it. The first picture opposite shows that stage of the manoeuvre.

When I watched the incident I assumed that the second beetle perched on the ball's top was the mate of the first; but I learned afterwards from pundits on dung-eaters that this was not the case. It was a pirate cadging a ride, with the intention of sharing the loot later. Doing no work either then or at any subsequent stage of the proceedings, it just balanced on the dung-top, looking rather like a performing seal riding a huge ball in a circus.

The working beetle pedalled the dung right across a hard-surfaced road to its soft-earthed edge. When the ball arrived there the creature resumed its normal stance, and began burrowing into the sandy soil below. Gradually it dug excavations round the sphere, which consequently started to subside into the ground. Then the beetle plunged into the loosened earth, and I could see from heaves, shifts and collapses of soil here and there that it was tunnelling immediately beneath the dung so as to ease its drop into a grave-like cavity. The ball sank steadily lower into the ground, as is shown in the pictures opposite. After half an hour of Herculean subterranean labour only a small fraction of it remained visible, and a few minutes later it disappeared altogether from view.

Most of that time the passenger beetle remained idle on the dung-heap, gradually descending with it like a miner starting to disappear down a mine-shaft.

In the mating season the females of some species deposit an egg in the centre of the dung-ball, so that when the grub hatches it is already provided with a ready-made larder full of food. Gradually the young beetles eat their way through those edible prison walls, and emerge into the outer world.

African Buffalo

Syncerus caffer

Buffaloes often wander about in considerable herds; and at Mara I once watched a party of as many as 600 grazing together. If unprovoked they are usually placid, mild-tempered and even rather shy creatures, belying their reputation for dangerous ferocity. Occasionally a human visitor can approach quite close to them as they sit lazily chewing the cud. No doubt they have self-confidence in their capacity for defence or offence if required.

Sometimes they appear to indulge in mock, make-believe aggressiveness. The herd pictured here was disturbed by the arrival of our land-rover as they fed in long grass in the country around Kiboko. After raising their heads and staring at us for a while, they advanced with a threatening air, like a platoon of soldiers marching against a foe. For some time they continued their determined approach—and then they all suddenly turned tail and ran away. At a few score yards distance they halted, faced us again, and advanced once more in solid, arrogant ranks—but again when they came within close hailing distance of us they pirouetted round, and galloped away. They repeated that performance four times, and it became more like a movement in a ballet than a tactic in a battle. Incidentally, it was obliging of the actors, for the sun kept disappearing behind clouds in a stormy sky, and opportunities for good colour photography were fitful.

If the movement was a deliberate feint, it was none the less based on formidable potentialities. Buffaloes can truly be among the most dangerous of all African game. Many an authority has told me that he would rather face an irate elephant than an angry buffalo. Especially if wounded, its charge is tempestuous as it races forwards grunting angrily, with its head defiantly upheld until it lowers the horns at the last moment to toss its victim like a vanquished toreador out of a bull-ring. In that situation usually only a well-placed bullet will halt it.

Its handsome, if diabolical, horns fit its head like a superlatively magnificent Viking's helmet. They make it a worthy match for its only natural enemy, the lion. When lions attack a herd of buffaloes the hunters prudently choose to go for a calf, or at most a cow. When thus threatened the buffaloes form themselves into a defensive semi-circle, with the cows and calves protected in its centre, and the bulls taking up positions on the exposed flanks. A duel between a veteran bull and a lion—or even two or three lions—is a prolonged as well as a bloody affair; and it is not always the buffalo that in the end succumbs. Many a lion has been slain in those engagements.

Dark-capped Bulbul

Pycnonotus xanthopygos

When I first arrived in Kenya I felt confused by the galaxy of strange birds which made themselves at home in my garden. I had never before set foot in Africa, and their appearances all seemed to me bafflingly exotic. It was true that some of their family names—such as dove, swallow and sunbird—were familiar, since I knew certain members of those tribes in other lands. But every individual species in Nairobi looked a distinct newcomer to me and I thought I should never meet a familiar feathered friend.

Then I heard a snatch of bird-song which was an echo from one of my previous existences. At once my memory transported me back to Malaya. Sure enough, looking into the tree whence the music came, I caught sight of a bulbul with a bright yellow patch beneath its tail reminiscent of the Yellow-vented Bulbul of Johore. Its size, figure and plumage appeared identical with those of that friendly creature, until I noticed that its head was blackish instead of the light grey of the Asian breed. Yet the similarity was sufficient to make me lose my sense of exile, and to make me, too, begin to feel at home in my new African garden.

The bird was the Dark-capped Bulbul of Africa; and a recognised alternative name for it is the Yellow-vented Bulbul. It is a close relative of its kinsman living several thousand miles away on the opposite shores of the Indian Ocean. Not only in appearance and voice, but also in cheerful, vivacious habits it is like that other common garden bird. I have read that one of its popular melodious phrases is interpreted by the words, 'Back to Calcutta— back to Calcutta'; but that must be a misinterpretation. I have seen red-vented, red-whiskered and white-cheeked bulbuls in Bengal, but so far as I know no Yellow-vented Bulbuls reside there. The correct interpretation of the Kenya species' call must be 'Back to Malaysia'.

Since those first days in Nairobi I have, of course, discovered many other species of birds closely related to well-known characters on distant continents. There are various kinds not only of doves, swallows and sunbirds, but also of crows, orioles, plovers, night-jars, eagles, owls, herons, shrikes and other types which I know in Europe, Asia, America or Australasia. But except for some migrants, few of them are the same identical species. That is notable evidence of the abundant variety of Nature all round the world. Yet one very interesting circumstance is that different species on widely separated continents which belong to the same family almost always share the same particular inherited customs in their courtship, nest-building, incubation and other bird behaviour—as I shall describe later.

The picture of a Dark-capped Bulbul on the opposite page is rather more than life-size, for the actual bird measures about seven inches long.

Kori Bustard

Ardeotis kori

An adult male of these giants among East African bustards stands about four feet high. Like most other members of the various local species of bustards, it is a bird of open country. Largely earth-bound—for it seems rather reluctant to fly—it walks with stately tread across the land; and it is a great benefactor of agriculture, for it greedily destroys locusts as well as numerous sorts of other insects, molluscs, small reptiles and various kinds of vegetable matter, including weed-seeds.

At the appearance of a human being its behaviour is erratic, sometimes betraying shyness as it runs away with crouching gait in efforts at concealment, and at other times demonstrating fearless curiosity as its stands its ground and stares back at the intruder. When it resorts to flight its wing-beats are slow, deliberate and powerful.

Kori Bustards are fairly common in Kenya. I have come across them in various regions, sometimes singly or in pairs, and at other times in parties of up to a dozen birds of both sexes. The portrait opposite shows a cock in all his handsome plumage. He exploits that adornment with extraordinary effect when displaying to a desirable hen in the mating season. I have gazed in wonder at those antics, scarcely able to believe my eyes at his strange contortions. First he stretches himself as tall and stiff as a fence-pole; then he tips his outspread tail upright against his back; and afterwards he inflates all the feathers on his neck until they form a fluffy white balloon into which his head almost completely disappears. The bustard seems to have turned itself partly inside out; and if glimpsed suddenly in that posture it is almost unrecognisable as a bird at all. Nor is this the end of its performance, for in that fabulous stance it turns from side to side—as if it were a contortionist-conjurer inviting an audience to inspect every aspect of his body to try to discover where all its members have disappeared. Then it struts a few sedate paces forward, and finally halts in transfixed stiffness again. The cock's only audience is usually in fact a hen of his own species, who is apparently so overcome with admiration and emotion at his act that she promptly submits herself to his will. They mate then and there.

The eventual result of that last magical conjuring trick performed by both of them jointly is a brace of streaked and mottled brown eggs laid on bare ground, from which in due course two fluffy chicks emerge.

This and other extravagant courtship displays are characteristic of the cocks among most of the various large bustard species scattered widely across the world.

White-bellied Bustard

Eupodotis senegalensis

About a dozen different species of bustards are found in East Africa. The White-bellied Bustard is one of the smaller types; and it has the same sort of stately walk when relaxed, the same shy instinct for concealment when first disturbed, and the same serene, dignified stance when its confidence has been restored, as most of its relations.

The bird shown here was the father in a family party of parents and youngsters which we came across one morning in the wilds of Kiboko during the first few days of May. As usual in such circumstances, the group consisted of a quartet: a mama, a papa, and two half-grown youngsters. They were all busily feeding in grasses taller than their own approximately two-foot-high selves; and it was difficult to secure photographs of them as they crouched nervously or ran skulking through the undergrowth in attempts to escape our attentions. But after a while they grew accustomed to us, seemed to accept that we were harmless if grotesque passers-by, and resumed their searches for the insects which they were hunting. After that one or two of them occasionally posed obligingly in open spaces, where they halted to gaze at us inquisitively for a few fleeting seconds in between bouts of pecking at the ground. An instant later they would disappear again behind tall grasses, chasing energetically after further prey. They were for ever on the move, scarcely hesitating for a fraction of a moment except to capture a fresh morsel of food, to scratch a ticklish feather—or to eye us slightly suspiciously every time that the camera shutter clicked as it took another picture. Between them the quartet must have eaten hundreds of insects every hour.

Like other bustards, they are distinct benefactors of mankind, for their choicest food is locusts. In the merry springtime each pair lays its two eggs on bare, open ground, making no attempt to cup them in any sort of nest. Usually the clutch comes to no harm, and between March and June family parties such as the one we saw are common all over Kenya's plains.

Serval Cat

Felis serval

The cat tribe in Africa boasts such splendid creatures as the Lion, the Leopard, and the Cheetah. Yet no member of the company is more attractive than the Serval Cat. Smaller than any of the trinity mentioned above, and larger than several other members of the clan such as the Caracal, a full-grown specimen stands some twenty inches high, stretches about fifty-four inches long, and weighs approximately thirty-four pounds. Its big upstanding ears, small kittenlike face, lanky athletic legs, and tawny-yellow coat splashed all over with black spots could scarcely be more handsome judged by the most exacting standards of feline pulchritude.

A nocturnal hunter, the Serval Cat preys on guinea-fowl and other birds, cane rats, hares, small antelope fawns, and similar victims. Being a night prowler, it is not often visible to man except in the very early mornings or the late afternoons; and even then its appearances are fleeting, for it usually dwells in thick undergrowth, and leaps quickly into cover when detected.

How, then, were the cats on the opposite page persuaded to pose for their portraits?

A litter of serval kittens often numbers three; and one day near Maralal such a trio of almost new-born youngsters was found abandoned in their cradle, an old ant-bear's burrow. They were helpless, since their mother had apparently been killed. Their discoverer rescued them, and presented them to Group-Captain and Mrs. Barrett, who ranched in the neighbourhood, and whose fond skill at rearing wild animals was well known. The cats shown here were two of that family at the age of seven months.

At the Barretts' house they were not confined to a cage or enclosure. Only at nights were they induced indoors for safety, and fed on raw meat. Being orphans with no tutor of their own kind to train them, they had not yet learned to hunt; but they were in process of teaching themselves. Throughout each day the world around the house was theirs to explore at random, for they were let out-of-doors at dawn, and left free until evening to go wherever they chose. They romped through wild bush beyond the garden, but usually came running home at a call from one of their human guardians.

They regarded the Barretts as their foster-parents, but did not always treat them with the awed respect due to occupants of that station. Before leaving the house at the start of a new day they would visit them in their bedroom, jump on to their beds, and sometimes upset their cups of early morning tea all over the bedclothes before waving a friendly 'good-bye' with their frisky paws, and leaping through the windows into the sunlight beyond.

Cheetah

Acinonyx jubatus

If I had to decide which is my favourite animal in all the splendid menagerie of Kenya's wilds, I should consider carefully the varied rival claims of half-a-dozen close contestants for that supreme distinction, and probably finally select the cheetah. It would owe this choice to its combination of qualities: an elegant athletic figure, lovely grace of movement, brilliant accomplishment as a hunter, and a rather unshy, nonchalant and at the same time enigmatic character.

The photographs on the opposite pages show the beast's beauty of form and colour. They display, too, its proud bearing, and give a hint of its relaxed self-confidence and fearlessness. But what motionless pictures like these cannot convey is its terrific turn of speed. The cheetah is the fastest animal on land, its sprint attaining a speed of about sixty miles per hour. Certain birds can far exceed that pace. Swifts for example sometimes touch 125 m.p.h. when hunting, whilst a peregrine falcon swoops after its prey at 160 miles an hour. But on ground the cheetah probably holds the record.

European travellers first became acquainted with cheetahs in eighteenth-century India at the courts of the Mogul Emperors, where they were trained to hunt gazelles and black-buck for their royal masters. In those days these great felines were common residents in India and some Near Eastern countries; but now they have almost disappeared from those lands and are plentiful only in Africa.

The cheetah's technique of hunting is unique among catlike creatures. Its slim, lithe, long-legged figure is built for speed. First it stalks conveniently close to its prey, and then it races full-tilt at the victim. Relying less on the furtive stalk than on that burst of speed, it does not need to allow time for acceleration, since its initial velocity at its first leap is tremendous. Shooting forward like an arrow from a bow, it has been timed to attain a speed of fifty-four m.p.h. within three seconds of standing motionless. And it can maintain its top-sprint pace for rather more than a hundred yards. If it does not reach its target within that space of ground, it abandons the chase, and—short of wind from the effort— lies panting in the grass to recover breath.

Usually, however, it judges a distance nicely, catches up with its victim, leaps at the hapless creature, seizes it by the throat, and kills it by strangulation. On East Africa's plains the usual prey are impalas and gazelles, though a cheetah sometimes goes for females or young of the larger antelopes, and even for a zebra or wildebeest. If it is very hungry it satisfies itself with smaller game like warthogs, hares, guinea-fowls or infant ostriches. Customarily a cheetah hunts alone or in a pair, but sometimes a small party of anything up to half-a-dozen works as a team. The first picture (opposite) shows a couple eyeing a herd of gazelles just before giving chase, and the second (overleaf) shows a trio relaxing after a meal.

One of the intriguing facts about this great hunter is that it can fairly easily be tamed. I have already referred to its training for sports pursued by the Mogul princes of old. Often in modern times cheetahs have been induced to become even more domesticated than that as household pets. They develop then the mild, gentle and even affectionate side of their natures; and when stroked the beast purrs like a cat, though with a somewhat harsher tone. It looks a startlingly dramatic companion sitting beside its owner on a drawing-room sofa!

Nevertheless, I feel dubious about its merits in such circumstances. Mr. Armand Denis, whose friendly knowledge of cheetahs as pets is unsurpassed, and whose high admiration for the handsome creature is sincere, nevertheless declares that as a domestic companion it is 'stupid, indifferent, obstinate and hopelessly uncooperative'.* In addition I suspect that it can be unreliable. I would never completely trust it. That is not because of any fault in its own character, but because of the risk of a sudden tragic misunderstanding with some uncomprehending human being. A cheetah can be skittish, and in playful mood it might start one of its brisk sprints at a casual visitor to a house. Naturally that individual might be startled, mistake the mock aggression for a real attack, and take defensive action. Misunderstanding breeds misunderstanding, and the cheetah might feel itself threatened, and promptly change its mood from fun to fury. Such an accident could happen especially with children untutored in the ways of wild animals.

At one time I toyed with the idea of keeping two or three cheetahs at large in my garden at Government House. They would have added superbly to the decorativeness of its spacious lawns, lovely flower-beds, and blossoming shrubberies. But many children came to enjoy those gracious static amenities, and I would not have liked any sudden, fatal disturbance of their enjoyment by a less static attraction to occur.

I have written that cheetahs are plentiful in Africa. In most of Kenya's nature reserves tourists can see them more easily than leopards, for example, partly because they are diurnal rather than nocturnal hunters, and partly because they are less shy than those other cats. Nevertheless, they are declining in numbers. The reason may be that since human settlement spread over very wide areas in East Africa, and as a consequence the regions where wild animals roamed freely became more limited, those regions have shrunk too small for cheetahs to breed in sufficient numbers to survive the rigours of nature. That is a serious consideration, needing most careful thought and action; for it would be deplorable if the most beautiful of all Africa's wild beasts disappeared from the face of the Earth.

* In an article in the magazine *Animals*.

Red-knobbed Coot

Fulica cristata

This species is distinguishable from the European Coot by two red knobs above the white shield on its forehead; but such identification is unnecessary in Kenya because the European bird is only a winter visitor to Africa which does not penetrate farther south than Khartoum.

On Lake Naivasha in June many clumps of reeds harbour floating Red-knobbed Coots' nests. When we visited the place towards the month's end most of them still contained clutches of eggs, and only in one had a solitary chick hatched. It squatted beside two unbroken eggs, looking as if it could not have emerged from its own shell more than a few moments earlier. Nevertheless at our approach it shuffled off the nest, jumped into the water, and swam away with the self-confidence of a champion swimmer. A parent promptly appeared from nowhere, and piloted it into concealment in another reed-clump nearby.

We photographed the owners of a nest containing the local record number of nine eggs— shown opposite. This involved cutting many tall reeds shielding the nest, so that the camera could gain an unobstructed view. The mother coot showed no undue alarm whilst we demolished the plants. Keeping an alert, cautious eye on us, she cruised around in the close vicinity without uttering any cries of protest or alarm. Within a minute of our withdrawal to a raft moored five yards away she returned and squatted on her prolific clutch. Evidently she did not approve of some of the minor adjustments which we had made to blades of the remaining reeds immediately around her nest, for she bent her head, gripped them in her beak, and rearranged them to her satisfaction. Otherwise she remained surprisingly unconcerned at the removal of a thick, hitherto concealing screen of rushes which had lent her privacy; and she settled down contentedly to her task of incubation.

Her mate stayed away from the nest longer, betraying the greater shyness which cock birds of many species show in such circumstances. But after a while he, too, swam back to the site, climbed on the nest beside her, and surveyed the prospect to assure himself that all was well. Later she rose and swam away whilst he settled on their eggs to do a turn of duty.

Other patches of reeds in the neighbourhood harboured nests of the coots' much more decorative relations, Purple Gallinules. These also contained eggs beneath sitting birds, and we intended to take their pictures. But unfortunately dark clouds suddenly flew across the sunny sky, and raindrops began to splash down before we could do so.

Red-knobbed Coots were very plentiful on the lake, sometimes swimming in close-packed fleets of several scores of birds together.

Long-tailed Cormorant
Phalacrocorax africanus

In the breeding season Lake Naivasha attracts many engaging types of water-birds, and throughout May, June and July a very populous nesting colony of them comes into existence on a group of dead trees half submerged in water. There African Spoonbills, Sacred Ibises, White-necked Cormorants, Long-tailed Cormorants, Darters, Large White Egrets, Black-headed and Buff-backed Herons, all build their nests, lay their eggs, and rear their young in an indiscriminate mob so messily overcrowded that in human terms the place would be described as a slum. No scene could be more hectically busy, for parent birds of every species keep flying to and fro, whilst the chicks of various types maintain a perpetual discordant chorus of cries for food. This extensive avian suburb of Naivasha township is raised amidst a peaceful prospect in which sparkling lake waters, green hills, blue-and-white skies, and bright sunshine co-operate to compose a landscape of idyllic beauty. In June the lake's surface is plentifully sprinkled with blue water-lilies, and among them swim flotillas of gulls, pelicans, coots, grebes, ducks and various other birds, as well as the residents of the nesting colony.

The Long-tailed Cormorant is considerably smaller than its White-necked cousin (who will appear overleaf), measuring two feet long, or slightly less, in comparison with the other's three feet. Additional distinguishing features are its ruby-red eyes, and its plumage, which is uniformly velvety-black except for silver-grey patches on the wings. Finally—as its name indicates—its tail is longer in proportion to the rest of its body than is that of the related species.

Otherwise the bird displays the same cormorantish figure and behaviour—swimming, diving, and chasing after fish and frogs underwater most of every day. A bird engaged on one of those forays is shown on the opposite page.

In flight Long-tailed Cormorants have something of the appearance of wild duck, speeding forward with rapid wing-beats, and rarely leaving the immediate vicinity of water. Thus, when flying along a zig-zag river a flock will usually keep to the channel's winding course, following exactly its every twist and turn instead of taking short cuts overland. The habit may be due to the birds' instinctive disinclination to risk assault by hostile hawks away from the protective element of water. If such a foe appears as they travel high above a river, pond or lake, the cormorants promptly drop with great splashes into the water, and disappear from view below its surface.

White-necked Cormorant

Phalacrocorax lucidus

Like all cormorants, this is a masterly angler depending for its existence wholly on its skill at catching fish. Neither it nor its youngsters eat anything else; and so their nests are always lodged in trees, bushes or other eminences above water, where they are surrounded by multitudes of their prey.

Sometimes these Cormorants fish by cruising amidst water-plants on a lake's surface and dipping their faces to catch their lively food lurking among the weeds; but usually they engage in deep-water fishing. From a submarine observation tank at Mzima Springs in Tsavo I once watched that exciting sport. The pool's surface appeared half-way up the plate-glass window through which I gazed; and so I could see the upper and lower portions of a cormorant above and below water respectively as it floated around in a preliminary reconnaissance. Its webbed feet paddled slowly forwards, its neck was held erect, and its harpoon-beaked head gazed expectantly downwards. Suddenly it dipped its face beneath the water, and I watched its wide-open eyes inspect aquatic society spread below. Then with a quick backwards thrust of both legs its body tilted upside-down in a half-somersault, and a moment later the bird shot through the water in an unswerving straight line to the pool's sandy floor. As it descended a long string of bubbles, like a necklace of silvery beads, escaped from its plumage and rose airily to the surface above. All the time the bird held its neck at full stretch, with its beak pointed downwards like a dagger; and now and then it turned its head from side to side as it peered keenly this way and that. It stayed underwater a long time, travelling considerable distances, and often changing direction by a quick thrust of a foot. Unfortunately clumps of water-weeds sprouting from the pool's bed sometimes obscured my view; and I never saw it actually make a catch. But once I glimpsed it with a small fish gripped across its bill, which it manipulated so as to arrange the food conveniently for swallowing. But before it completed that operation it suddenly darted off in another direction out of my sight, hunting along a new trail. And soon afterwards I saw it shoot swiftly upwards, break the pool's surface, and float serenely there with a much larger fish held in its beak. It swallowed that captive in one gulp. Had it first eaten the little fish below water, and then a bigger prize in the air above?

It enjoyed good hunting that morning, for a few minutes later I saw it with a foot-long eel wriggling in its bill. The bird had a difficult job arranging that reluctant tit-bit conveniently for gobbling; but in the end it succeeded.

Lake Naivasha

The picture opposite shows part of the colony of breeding birds on Lake Naivasha which I have already described. They build their myriad nests all over a group of tall dead trees standing half drowned in several feet of water. On the otherwise bare branches of that arbour the birds' nests sprout like fantastic foliage with lively flowers which are cormorants, darters, ibises, spoonbills, egrets and herons. Swimming among water-lilies sprinkling the lake below are wild duck, grebes, coots, gulls, pelicans and various other types of birds. The scene composes a fabulous sort of botanical garden.

One reason why Kenya possesses such large numbers of different birds, beasts, fish and other animals is the remarkable variety of its terrains and climates. They vary from hot, humid tropical sea-shores along the coast to eternally snow-capped Mount Kenya in its interior; from closely settled farmlands in its dramatically undulating highlands to vast, flat, sparsely populated regions of pasture lands; and from great stretches of bushy savannah or lush forest to boundless areas of arid desert. These cause an ever-changing succession of landscapes, and their varied picturesqueness is sometimes enhanced by original touches added by the wild animals who live among them. The nesting colony of water-birds at Naivasha is one example of that.

Herds of elephants in places like Tsavo Park provide another. Elephants are both grazers and browsers, with a catholic taste which makes them eat innumerable kinds of grasses, leaves and fruits of shrubs and trees. Incidentally their resultant capacity to exist in all sorts of country is one reason why they have survived in goodly numbers the persecutions of hunters seeking their ivory tusks, in contrast to rhinoceroses, whose feeding grounds are much more limited, and whose numbers have therefore been dangerously reduced by poachers coveting their horns. And since elephants' digestive organs are very inefficient, causing about half the vegetable matter swallowed by them to be wasted, the giants over-eat on a grand scale. In their zeal to enjoy succulent leaves growing near tree-tops they uproot whole trees; and a hungry herd will demolish entire copses as their meal proceeds. An area invaded by them often looks like a graveyard of trees when they depart. They strip not only branches of their foliage, but also trunks of their bark; and the wooden skeletons lie tumbled everywhere in attitudes of abandon like an exhibition of modern abstract sculptures.

White-browed Coucal

Centropus superciliosus

This bird is best known by its call—a bubbling cry which has been likened to water pouring from a bottle, and which has therefore earned it the nickname 'Water-bottle Bird'. Often that vocal ejaculation is the first warning one receives of a White-browed Coucal's presence within a few yards, for it usually skulks in thick cover in the dense bush country which it inhabits. Behaving like a rodent rather than a bird, it walks more often than it flies, creeping around in tangled grass, thickets and other wild undergrowth as it hunts its prey. Only periodically does it rise, hop by hop, from branch to branch through a shrub, until it surfaces for a short while on the open summit before plunging down again into the jungly depths below. It is partial to waterside resorts, where it tunnels its way through rank reed-beds, marshy vegetation and tall elephant grass. No doubt those habits are due to the fact that it gorges itself on large insects, reptiles and mice.

Though related to the cuckoos, none of the several different species of coucals in East Africa is parasitic. On the contrary, White-browed Coucals are devoted, dutiful parents. Their nests are large, loose, untidy structures woven of grass stalks, twigs and leaves, and shaped like oval balls, sometimes coated with thin interlacing branches as extra protection on their exteriors. A hole is situated on one side as an entrance; and the clumsy edifice is hidden in thick cover a few feet from the ground. Both birds in a pair help to incubate their customary quartet of eggs; and they are afterwards conscientious guardians, feeders and tutors of the chicks. Indeed, it is said that when threatened by grass-fires or other perils the adult birds transport their young to security by carrying them, woodcock-fashion, between their thighs to a new home a safe distance away. They are indeed model parents, beyond reproach.

Two-Banded Courser

Hemerodromus africanus

The bird pictured opposite sat on a solitary egg in the middle of a roadway at Tsavo. Tourist traffic used the road frequently, as was shown by a pair of deeply impressed tyre tracks running along the centre of its gravelly surface. The courser's egg lay within two feet of one of those grooves, exposed on the bare highway with no protection except its own cunning camouflage colouring.

The bird's plumage also had good protective colouring, which evidently gave it a considerable instinctive sense of security, for it was not easily alarmed. On separate occasions I watched two motor-cars and a bus pass about a foot away from it. Each time the little courser sat completely unruffled until the huge vehicle seemed almost on top of it. Then it fluffed out its feathers in protest, rose, scurried a few yards off, stood watching the now fast receding intruder, and a moment later hastened back to settle again on its precious egg.

When we halted our land-rover five yards away our probably unprecedented stop alarmed the sitting bird. It jumped up, ran quickly into long grass beside the road, and stayed hidden there for a quarter of an hour. Then rain began to fall, and almost immediately it reappeared and stood staring at us suspiciously, obviously wondering whether it could return to act as an umbrella for its egg. It remained undecided for nearly ten minutes, but advanced gradually in a series of short runs and long halts. First it hastened three or four paces forwards, then it stood stock still for quite a while, afterwards it moved onward another few steps, then it stayed motionless for a couple of minutes, then it walked another inch or two nearer—and so on, until at last it arrived beside the egg, glanced down at it with satisfaction, and squatted on it.

We made no movement for some time, to let it recover a sense of tranquillity. When Chris's camera then clicked, the bird showed no particular concern, merely glancing up at us as if intrigued by some new, strange sound in Nature. When the noise was repeated shortly afterwards it did not even bother to look in our direction. In fact it became too completely indifferent to the busily snapping camera, sitting phlegmatically motionless, and becoming a dull model. Chris wanted it to look this way and that, to stand up and sit down again, or to give some other interesting performance. So I cautiously opened the car door, and stepped down on the roadway in the hope of disturbing it just a little, but not too much. That was more than the bird could tolerate. It rose hurriedly, took to its wings, and flew far across the surrounding grass.

Ten minutes later we saw it returning towards us by a series of runs and hesitations along the road; but it stopped twenty yards away and stayed there for the next hour, eyeing us with fixed suspicion. Now and then other cars trundled by within a foot or two of its egg; but it refused to come and have its photograph taken.

84

Crowned Crane
Balearica regulorum

As the frontispiece to this book indicates, Crowned Cranes are perhaps the most decorative large birds in Kenya. And as you can see here, the cock and the hen appear alike. So among these beauties each sex is the fair sex.

Usually they lay their eggs on wide platforms of reeds trampled down by the birds themselves amidst swamps. Each year a couple do that on a reed-bed in a pool below the Treetops Hotel in the Aberdares forest. I watched them one afternoon when their two nestlings were only a quarter grown, but large enough to venture with the parents on foraging expeditions. The family were stalking with long-legged elegance and greedy preoccupation beside the pool—when a herd of elephants entered the scene from the surrounding woodland.

For some reason the leading bull elephant was in a bad temper. He came into the open ground trumpeting furiously, as if he must be suffering from some intolerable tooth (or tusk) ache. Catching sight of a party of waterbucks resting beside the pool, he rushed at them and chased them away. Observing some baboons gambolling nearby, he forced them also to retreat. Then he did the same to two bushbucks.

At that point he noticed the Crowned Cranes strolling around. Taking umbrage at their indifference to his lordly presence, he advanced hostilely towards them, with several of his elephantine comrades supporting him. They composed an array of unfriendly Titans formidable enough to panic an army. But not a Crowned Crane! One of the adult birds raised its head and stared at the elephants defiantly as it uttered warning calls to its mate and chicks. That trio gathered behind it and, evidently on its advice, began a gradual retreat. The bull elephant advanced within a few yards of the guardian bird, raised his trunk, trumpeted vociferously, and spread his vast ears sideways in the gesture often preliminary to a charge. But the crane stood its ground as its family withdrew, honking aloud protestingly, opening its wings, and waving them vigorously as if in imitative retort to the tormentor's ear flappings. I thought the elephant would attack; but the bird's retaliation seemed to impress it, for it moved only two more paces forward, and then stood screaming, still with outflung ears and trunk. Slowly the gallant crane began to retire backwards, facing its foe all the time, and maintaining cries of protest—rather like Horatius keeping the enemy at bay on his famous bridge. The bird did not hurry, its pace being dictated by the inability of its chicks to walk faster. And as it withdrew the group of elephants advanced with equal slowness, seeming to judge that in the circumstances discretion was the better part of valour.

It was an engaging confrontation between one David and a troop of Goliaths.

Crocodile

Crocodylus niloticus

Our present-day crocodiles appear fearsome enough; but they are mere pigmies compared with their ancestors of prehistoric times. Those monsters' fossilised remains show that they had skulls measuring six feet long, and a total body length of about fifty feet. They cannot have been pleasant creatures to meet on a dark night.

When a female crocodile wishes to spawn she leaves her river or lake, wanders overland to a sandy spot, scrapes holes in the earth there, deposits numerous eggs in these, and covers them up again. Then she remains on the nest pit during the approximate ninety days incubation period, perhaps without feeding, and often in a state of torpor. When her youngsters are ready to hatch they give a signal by 'quacking' inside their shells, a sound loud enough to be audible through the eggs and several inches of earth. The mother promptly digs up her clutch, and each young croc escapes from confinement by cutting through its shell with a weapon provided by Nature for that purpose—an 'egg-tooth' growing on its snout. When the infant emerges it is already perfectly formed—a miniature dragon measuring some eight inches long, with snapping jaws, flicking tail and wiggling feet, capable of walking, swimming, fighting and feeding itself.

Careful records indicate that an average clutch laid by a female contains between fifty and sixty eggs. That rate of reproduction would hugely overstock the waters of East Africa with crocodiles if more than a tiny fraction of the ferocious little reptiles survived their infancy. But in fact an overwhelming majority of them—perhaps about forty-nine out of every fifty!—live scarcely more than a few minutes. In Kenya they have two deadly enemies. The first is the Monitor Lizard, which hunts for buried crocodiles' eggs, unearths them in hordes, smashes their shells, and swallows the contents; and the second is the Marabou Stork. That bird waits until the baby crocodiles hatch, and then grabs them galore either as they scamper over the ground towards the near-by lake or river, or just as they start to swim in its shallows.

Sometimes a parent crocodile tries to prevent this latter massacre of the innocents. Lurking in deeper water, it advances furtively towards a murderous stork, and suddenly snaps at it. But the wily bird sees the croc coming, and side-steps every attack. Nevertheless, it is perhaps those vain attempts to kill the storks which succeed in ensuring that a sufficient quantity of the new crocodile generation survives, for whilst the bird is side-stepping its assailant one or two youngsters escape into the water. So the over-all crocodile population remains steady.

The picture opposite shows an example of peaceful co-existence between crocodiles and Goliath Herons on the shores of Lake Baringo.

Spotted Stone Curlew

Burhinus capensis

This is a most cautious bird. Knowing that, when we found a nest at Maralal I went three hours ahead of Chris to erect a hide, in the hope that the curlews would become used to that intruder before her photography began.

When I appeared one bird was sitting on the two eggs, whilst the other stood companionably beside it. They both promptly fled. Ten minutes after I had established myself in the hide they emerged from bushes forty yards away. Venturing two or three very cautious steps at a time between long nervous halts, they gradually approached the nest, but finally stopped fifteen yards from it. One behind the other they then turned and started a slow-march reconnaissance in a complete circle round the nest and the hide, inspecting the latter from every angle. During the next two hours they performed three such inspection tours, each at an excruciatingly cautious, funereal pace.

One bird did occasionally venture nearer than their fifteen yards encircling perimeter. Step by step, with long hesitations between each greatly daring footfall, it came to within five feet of its eggs—and then took fright, turned tail, and ran back to its timidly waiting mate. Four times it repeated that act, always with the same anti-climax.

Two hours and two minutes (to be exact) after my erection of the hide the bolder bird took a sudden firm decision. Strolling deliberately to the nest, it sat down on the eggs. I heaved a silent sigh of relief. But soon afterwards the curlew lost confidence again, rose hastily, and skedaddled away to rejoin its mate. In the next half-hour it repeated its nervous advances and retreats five times without ever quite reaching the eggs. At its sixth attempt, however, it was just about to settle on them—when a land-rover hove in sight with Bill Langridge, Rodney Elliott and Chris. Both birds fled helter-skelter out of sight.

They stayed invisible until ten minutes after Chris was installed. Then they re-emerged from hiding, and for the next two hours performed again all their earlier tantalising reconnaissances, advances and withdrawals. At last one of them again took a firm decision, walked to the nest, and sat down. Chris snapped a photograph, and the bird immediately rose and raced away. But it was now gradually acquiring courage, and after three more experimental jaunts close to the eggs, followed by retreats, at the fourth venture it settled on them. As it lowered its body over them Chris took another snapshot—and it continued lowering its body, unperturbed. But the noise of her winding the next exposure was too much for it. Jumping up in panic, it sprinted away.

After that both birds became even shyer, and for hours neither of them came near the nest. We departed, leaving the hide in position. By next morning they were accustomed to it; and they cooperated perfectly with the photographer.

African Darter

Anhinga rufa

A darter is distinguishable from a cormorant by its longer and thinner neck culminating in a slimmer head and a straight, sharp-pointed (instead of hooked) beak. Its appearance from the shoulders upwards is therefore distinctly snake-like. That similarity is accentuated when the bird swims, for it sinks the rest of its body below water, and speeds forward with only its long neck and narrow head protruding. So it appears like a miniature—but far from mythical—Loch Ness monster; and this apparition gives the African Darter, like all other darters round the world, the popular name of 'Snake-bird'.

In Kenya it frequents every lake, swamp and river where open water and ample fish or frogs provide its requirements; and it sometimes also visits sheltered bays, inlets and river estuaries along the coast. The bird shown here was a resident in the colony of nesting birds at Lake Naivasha which I have already mentioned. Several darters had eggs or nestlings in that populous, noisy community; and they appeared more highly strung and nervous at our arrival in a small boat than any of the half-dozen other species of local inhabitants. As soon as we approached a darters' nest the adult birds on it would writhe their necks in excited, snaky motions for a few moments, then leap frantically into the water, and dive out of sight. The more grown-up youngsters followed suit, jumping into the lake with the abandon of would-be suicides plunging to their deaths. Younger nestlings also sometimes left their nests, clambering desperately away in search of safety through the surrounding tangle of branches. They were all as panicky as could be.

Not long afterwards the birds which had dived into the lake reappeared here and there above its surface, with only their long necks and slim heads emerging, like a school of sea-serpents. As often as not they sank again as soon as they saw our boat cruising around. If we moved away a little, however, their confidence was in due course restored, and they would then surface beside their nest trees, climb out on to a bending branch, and ascend laboriously, step by step and flutter by flutter, to their homes. Their balance on the thin lengths of wood was precarious, and it took them a long time to arrive at their destinations; but for some reason they preferred that method of progress to flying straight from the water back to their nurseries.

The nests were broad, untidy platforms of interlacing sticks balanced in nooks and crannies of the trees; and on each of them a clutch of between two and five eggs had been laid. In comparison with the mostly black plumage of their parents, the nestlings were clad in infantile white down and feathers.

Kirk's Dik-dik

Rhynchotragus kirkii

This exceedingly small and enchantingly graceful antelope stands approximately fourteen inches high at its shoulders. Kirk's Dik-dik—the commonest species through most of Kenya—is about the smallest antelope on Earth, being comparable with the various Pigmy Antelopes. In long grass it is virtually invisible, betraying its presence only by the waving of the grass-stalks as it strolls or bounds friskily forwards. When it reveals itself the short horns of the male, the longish, sensitive, proboscis-like nose on both sexes, and their gently contemplative eyes are particularly noticeable features of animals which in every aspect and movement are pleasing. They are rarely met in larger companies than a devoted pair. Periodically that pair will of course produce a youngster; but the fond parents conceal and guard it so jealously that it is hardly ever seen.

Dik-diks of this or that sub-species are widespread in various parts of Kenya. They are mostly browsers eating leaves and berries, although sometimes they also dig up roots for consumption. Able to exist for indefinite periods without drinks of water, they inhabit semi-arid as well as more sumptuous regions. And although they are shy, they also appear to be inquisitive. Often if you come upon a dik-dik suddenly beside a road in daylight, or catch sight of it along the beams of a car's headlights by night, it will stand unstirring for a long while, gazing in wonder at the four-wheeled monster unexpectedly invading its territory. It is then the personification of prettiness.

But dik-diks need to be cautious, because they have many enemies. The larger birds of prey in the sky overhead, and the smaller predators on land all around are very partial to their flesh. For example, I have seen a cemetery of bones of the animal's severed limbs lying beneath a tree occupied by a Bateleur Eagles' nest; and I have also watched a Silver-backed Jackal carrying a dik-dik captive in its mouth. Indeed, I have observed a couple of those cunning jackals at Uaso Nyiro who, hunting in partnership, each caught at the same time one of a pair of dik-diks. The tasty little beasts are a favourite dish of various other carnivores too.

The animals in the pictures here are demonstrating their characteristic curiosity whilst Chris takes their photographs. The upper portrait shows the hornless female, which is always slightly larger than the male; whilst the lower one reveals a fond pair hesitating for a while before taking to their heels in flight at the click of her camera.

94

African Hunting Dog

Lycaon pictus

The African Hunting Dog, popularly known as the Wild Dog, is a unique species. About the size of an Alsatian, it is more slenderly and wirily built, and has more formidable jaws and a much more forbidding appearance than that other clever creature. Perhaps this is not surprising, since it is the most relentless hunter in the African wilds.

Frequenters of spacious, bushy plains, Wild Dogs do not stalk their prey furtively like lions, but chase them openly; and they do not hunt individually or in small family parties like cheetahs, but collaborate in packs varying from half-a-dozen to forty beasts. Their favourite victims are speedy animals like impalas, gazelles and other antelopes; and they pursue them with intelligent, well-organised strategical and tactical co-operation. I have occasionally watched hunting parties on the job. First the team selects which individual in a distant grazing herd they will destroy; and then they give chase to it. One or two members of the pack start towards it at a tremendous pace, so manœuvring that their victim-to-be becomes detached from its companions and darts away in solitary flight. The other dogs trot behind them at a rather more comfortable, but still spanking pace, fanning out on either flank, and observing the pursuit eagerly—but biding their time. The race between the hunters and the hunted is well matched, for each is swift-moving; and as a spectacle it is all the more impressive because it is conducted in deathly silence, sometimes over miles of country. As the leading dog tires, it slackens pace. One of its supporters in the rear promptly breaks from a relaxed run into a fully extended sprint, and takes its place. So the chase continues like a relay race, with one fresh member of the dog team after another taking the position of leadership. Only the wretched antelope receives no relief, until eventually it tires and slackens pace. Then the whole mob of murderers catches up with it, closes on it, leaps at it, and takes vicious bites at it, until it falls to the ground from exhaustion and loss of blood. Within a few minutes little is left of it except a broken skeleton, for the dogs tear every hunk of flesh from its bones.

That is not a pretty picture; but many episodes in Nature are not pretty. Wild dogs play their allotted part in Creation's scheme of things. It is in some ways a useful and even an essential role. Probably it helps, for example, to ensure that the numbers of herbivores like impalas do not increase beyond quantities which healthy, periodically self-renewing vegetation can support.

Wild dogs sometimes drive lions and leopards from their kills. As for Man, though they have rarely been known to attack him, they are not shy of him, and will bark in fearless protest if he intrudes unduly on a scene. Accustomed to victory in all their contests, they possess supreme self-confidence.

Laughing Dove
Streptopelia senegalensis

Several pairs of Laughing Doves build nests in my garden. The photographs opposite illustrate a hazard attending their family life.

This nest was built in a flowering bougainvillea bush. Its two eggs hatched, and for three days afterwards the twin chicks squatted there whilst their parents took turns at sitting on them. Then one youngster disappeared, presumably kidnapped by some enemy. For the next five days the survivor continued to survive. Its down gradually gave way to quills, its quills began to burst into feathers, and it seemed so lusty that it would elude all the perils of infancy, and in due course leave home of its own volition.

Then the episode illustrated opposite occurred. During a two hours period whilst Chris sat in her hide taking photographs a Fiscal Shrike made five separate assaults on the nestling at moments when it was unattended by either of its parents. The shrike came furtively through the bougainvillea bush from behind. On four occasions Chris made sounds which frightened it away; but on the fifth she took this series of photographs. They show the sequence of events as follows:

1. a parent dove sitting on the youngster, ruffling its feathers at the approach of a shrike. (This picture was taken a few days earlier.)
2. the youngster sitting unprotected on the nest.
3. the shrike attacking from the left. It made a jab at the chick, and holds some captured fluff in its beak. The chick then backed away to the nest's further edge, and the shrike hopped through the bush and
4. attacked its victim from the right. After a brief struggle the youngster fell from the nest, and
5. the shrike pursued it as it tumbled through the bougainvillea. Chris hastened to its rescue, scared the shrike away, picked up the young dove from the ground, and replaced it on the nest, where soon afterwards
6. a parent bird returned to take care of it.

During the next two days I twice observed the shrike attack the nestling. Each time the youngster made defensive gestures; but probably it would have been destroyed if I had not driven the aggressor away. It grew in strength for two more days afterwards; and on the third morning the nest was empty. As I watched, a parent dove perched in the tree above the nest, and stayed there for a while. Then it flew to the nest to inspect it. Afterwards it fluttered to a bough overhead, and started coo-ing, as if it were calling for a youngster or its mate. Neither of them appeared.

Had the fledgeling flown of its own accord, or had their enemy at last bagged it?

Red-eyed Dove

Streptopelia semitorquata

In my brief essay about Dark-capped Bulbuls I mentioned that different species of birds belonging to the same family preserve similar domestic habits even when they live on separate, far-flung continents. They all inherit similar traditional tribal customs, so to speak.

A good example of that is provided by doves. Before I came to Africa I watched pairs of several diverse species of that family building nests in various parts of Europe and Asia; and I was always struck by their unanimous adoption of the same precise division of labour as they performed the task. One bird of a couple did all the selecting and fetching of building materials, whilst the other did all the fitting of those materials into their nest. The first would carefully choose suitable twigs and rootlets from trees and flowerbeds, and carry them to the second. That second bird sat tight all the time on the nest-to-be, never stirring, but receiving each bit of stuff from its mate and weaving it into its right place in the structure whilst the first dove sped away once more to fetch another piece. The pair repeated that act over and over again every few minutes, hour after hour and morning after morning, until the stick-platform which is their nest was firm enough to support a dove family for several weeks.

I was interested, therefore, to find that African doves go through exactly the same procedure. Two different species build nests in my garden in Nairobi, the Red-eyed Dove and the Laughing Dove; and both observe that identical, meticulous division of labour. Afterwards they produce the same customary number of eggs: two—never more and never less.

For that matter, all their conduct was precisely reminiscent of their various kinsmen in other parts of the world. Thus their courtship followed the same gallant manner. A cock Red-eyed Dove would puff out his chest and bow several times before his enchantress, emitting seductive coos as he did so—exactly as his Indian Little Brown Dove, his Malayan Spotted Dove, and his European Ring Dove counterparts all did. And the hen would respond with either the same slightly embarrassed indifference, or the same compliant curtsy as an introduction to mating—according to her mood—just as dove brides do in those other lands.

Similar comparisons can be made in the cases of other world-wide bird families. For instance, I shall describe later another remarkable example of such an identity of customs among the numerous sunbirds which are scattered across different continents.

The Red-eyed Dove illustrated here is a nestling still in its cradle; but it is almost ready to fly, and is exercising its wings in rehearsal for that great adventure.

White-faced Tree Duck

Dendrocygna viduata

The charming, alert, inquisitive group of characters pictured opposite is a typical glimpse of their kind. White-faced Tree Ducks are gregarious birds which congregate in parties of various sizes, some of their flocks at certain seasons of the year containing thousands of birds. When standing on dry land they hold themselves more erect than do other species of ducks; and they appear to be comparatively unshy (and perhaps rather stupid) creatures who are slow to take fright at the approach of a strange being. The small flock shown here in company with an egret seemed intrigued by our arrival in a land-rover twenty yards away from them beside a pond at Amboseli. When we halted they stayed stock still; when we approached closer to them they walked concernedly but reluctantly several paces away; and when we withdrew a short distance again they promptly retraced their steps back to their original position. When we stayed motionless there they also remained unmoving, staring at us as if dumbfounded by an astonishing spectacle.

Whether their title of Tree Duck is justified or not seems to be debatable. Some authorities declare that they occasionally settle in trees, whilst others assert that they never do. A nearly allied species in India certainly breeds in old stick nests abandoned by other birds on trees; and possibly this African type sometimes does likewise. In East Africa, however, they prefer to lay their clutches of between half-a-dozen and a dozen eggs either in a shallow, circular, scantily lined depression on dry ground, or else amidst thick reeds in deep water.

Because of their oft-reiterated clear whistle the species is sometimes called the Whistling Duck. No doubt one day a zealous ornithologist will devote himself to studying fully their family habits and history; and then I shall be able to write a longer essay about them.

Bateleur Eagle

Terathopius ecaudatus

The loftiest nest that Chris photographed during her visit to Kenya belonged to a family of Bateleur Eagles at Uaso Nyiro. Her hide was skied on top of a slim sixty-four-foot-high tower made of scaffolding poles; and how she sat cooped up there all day long for two successive days without either dizziness or panic is beyond my giddy, timid comprehension. The only creature that excelled her in patience was the bateleur nestling itself, which remained on its stick platform a few feet away for about four months.

Experts tell me that its portrait on the opposite page shows that it must have been about three months old when the picture was taken on June 3rd; and this reckoning is supported by the fact that Freddie Seed (who managed the Samburu Game Lodge close by) had first caught sight of it nearly two months earlier. Freddie supervised the building of a hide several days before Chris climbed to work there, so as to give the parent bateleurs time to become accustomed to its presence, and to resume unconcerned their regular visits with food for their youngster. On the day before Chris started photography, however, she and Freddie cut some branches and foliage surrounding the nest in order to expose it more clearly for her camera; and that interference with the surroundings must have caused the old bateleurs a fresh access of nervousness, for from the moment when Chris settled on her pinnacle at 6.45 the next morning until she descended toward dusk eleven hours later neither of them brought food to the nestling. That was not for want of trying on their parts, nor for lack of interest on the youngster's part, but resulted from their sheer fright about approaching the nest.

All day I watched the proceedings from concealment in the middle of a thorn-bush 300 yards away. At 8.45 a.m.—two hours after our arrival on the scene—the hen bateleur soared for a while high in the sky above the nest; but she made no attempt to descend, perhaps merely conducting a preliminary reconnaissance. At 10.30 she momentarily reappeared, this time much lower in the air. Ten minutes later the youngster on the nest started yelling, obviously demanding food; and a few seconds afterwards she flew purposefully to their home bough, alighted on it three feet from the nest, and dallied for a minute there. A long snake hung from her bill; and when she landed she transferred this to her talons, where she started tearing at it with her beak. Then she fluttered to another bough near by, perched on it facing her youngster, and continued to bite excitedly at the food. But after two minutes she picked up the mangled snake, and flew away with it.

Throughout that performance the nestling had uttered an almost continuous, ravenous cry for food; and it repeated its heartrending calls periodically throughout the next hour. All the time it (and I) could see its mother perched in a tree not far away, with the ration of snake still gripped beneath her feet. Occasionally she tore at the food, but mostly she

gazed around the landscape, staring especially in the direction of the nest, obviously trying to pluck up courage to go and appease her offspring's hunger. Once during that period the cock bird appeared overhead with a scrap of food dangling from his talons. He flew close by the nest, and for a moment I thought he would land there; but then he suddenly changed his mind, veered away, mounted high in the sky, and disappeared.

At last, at 11.30 a.m., the hen summoned up resolution, and flew to the nest-edge with the hunk of snake hanging from her bill. Alighting beside the youngster, she stayed there only between ten and twenty seconds before flying off again—without having delivered her gift. She went to the bough a few feet away where she had perched briefly before, and stayed there throughout the next half-hour tearing at her catch and gradually eating it herself. The youngster cried piteously the whole time, but failed to persuade her to return nearer. No doubt the sound of an occasional click from Chris's camera added to the mother's agitated nervousness.

During that half-hour the cock bateleur reappeared above the nest with food dangling from his claws. Circling round and round for nearly twenty minutes, he sometimes came quite near the home-tree, and at other times glided farther away. Eventually he descended almost to the nest, and I thought he was going to alight, when he hesitated abruptly in mid-air, flapped his wings vigorously in a braking action, and then turned and retreated to another tree not far away. A few minutes afterwards the female departed, having swallowed every bit of her snake, and having granted Chris the top picture on the opposite page just before taking wing.

The youngster continued to yell at its father. Soon that parent spread his wings again, glided deliberately low above the nest—almost as if he intended to air-drop the food there— and then slowly climbed higher into the sky and withdrew, still carrying his portion of the nestling's undelivered, belated breakfast. Some minutes later he changed his mind, cruised back once more over the nest with the food now gripped in his beak—but again failed in resolution, turned tail, and finally disappeared beyond a distant horizon.

The youngster ceased calling for food as soon as both parents had faded from view; and for the first time in almost two hours silence descended on the frustrating scene.

No adult bateleur reappeared until about 2 p.m., when the hen flew high above the nest. At once the youngster became excited, and called raucously; but its mother took no discernible notice, and departed as rapidly as she had come. Nearly four hours later she put in another brief appearance, when the nestling again called loudly, though now half-heartedly; and once more the old bird made no response. Nothing further happened before we human beings packed up and took our leave as dusk began to fall.

Throughout those tedious hours of empty waiting the youngster mostly stood quietly on the nest, staring around at the outer world in all directions, no doubt keeping a hopeful look-out for any sign of an elder. Periodically it took a little exercise. First it would engage in a thorough preening of its feathers; then it would stretch its wings sideways, or sometimes above its back; and two or three times it flapped them quite energetically. On one occasion it even skipped a few hops into the air as it waved the wings, and then took a jump over the

nest edge on to the thick supporting bough. A moment later it jumped back into the nest. Those antics were probably some of its first practice lessons in the art of flying.

Only through the hottest middle hours of the day did it slouch down in the nest and indulge in a siesta.

I have no space here to record in detail the events of the following day. Suffice it to say that Chris settled in her hide at 6.30 a.m., and that throughout the next several hours each adult bird appeared at almost the exact times by the clock and the sun as on the previous day. On both her visits the mother bird (after twenty minutes hesitation in the first instance, and only a few minutes preliminary reconnaissance in the second) went to the nest and fed her youngster—as is shown in the lower picture on the previous page. The cock, on the other hand, again failed in resolution. Not only on his first arrival, but also at two subsequent sorties at roughly half-hour intervals, he flew quite close to the nest with food dangling from his beak, seemed on the point of landing there, and then took fright, and sheered off again. Perhaps because of his persistent timidity, and because she realised that their nestling was consequently going seriously short of food, the hen paid a third visit to the nest with an extra ration of snake at a few minutes past one o'clock. After that neither bird returned before sunset.

Bateleurs spend much of their time circling high in the sky, with masterful soaring flight. Their most customary call is a sharp barking shriek, sometimes of blood-curdling quality. They are capable of impressive aerial acrobatics, performing occasional somersaults like tumbler pigeons for example. When hunting they descend lower in the atmosphere, and proceed by alternate spasms of strong wing-flapping and serene gliding to scrutinise wide stretches of the earth below. Usually they do their own killing, and will tackle game up to the size of small antelopes; but they sometimes also feast on carrion, as is shown in the picture here of a Bateleur Eagle and a Tawny Eagle sharing a banquet together.

The young bateleur at Uaso Nyiro remained on its nest for another month after our visit; and Freddie reported that when it flew it continued for a further four months to depend on its parents for food. The family haunted a group of trees near its birthplace. Gradually the fledgeling learned to emulate its elders' magnificent powers of flight and hunting, and became an independent eagle capable of looking after itself.

Tawny Eagle

Aquila rapax

Africa is a continent very congenial to eagles and other birds of prey. In East Africa alone fourteen different species of eagles can be found, and the numbers of falcons, kites, buzzards, sparrow-hawks, harriers and allied types are considerably larger. Nine of the eagles proper stay as residents throughout the year, whilst the other five are seasonal visitors from Europe or Western Asia. Some of those migrants travel immense distances to winter in the African sunshine.

So Kenya's wide, vivid skies are often made more lively by the presence of one, two or more eagles circling high in the blue, peering downwards for glimpses of their prey. Common among them is the Tawny Eagle. The over-all colouring of its plumage can vary considerably from individual to individual, ranging from dark to pale brown. A specimen of the former variety is shown in the picture on the previous page. A rarer plumage phase, which occurs most frequently in north-eastern Kenya and Somaliland, is the light brownish-cream shown in the photograph opposite.

Usually Tawny Eagles are birds of the open plains, cultivated areas, and low hills; but at certain times of the year some resort to mountainous country. They hunt small mammals, lizards and large insects; but they are also fond of carrion. Leslie Brown has observed them feeding with Fish Eagles on dead flamingos;* and they sometimes associate with vultures and other scavengers at the remnants of lion or leopard kills, or with kites and similar refuse-grabbers round rubbish dumps in African villages or sportsmen's camps.

The picture on the previous page shows a Tawny Eagle sharing the former sort of feast with a Bateleur Eagle. Rodney Elliott and Chris had laid out a dead zebra in the hope of attracting a leopard within range of her camera as they sat patiently for hours on end in a leafy hide on a Maralal hilltop. But the only creatures drawn to the corpse that afternoon were two Bateleurs and three Tawny Eagles. Some vultures perching on surrounding tree-tops were tempted to descend to earth and help devour the spoil; but they were aware of the leopard's presence in undergrowth close by, and felt nervous lest the beast should take offence at their thieving, and pounce on them. So they prudently stayed aloft. Their judgement was sound. After a while the leopard made a sudden appearance—and instantaneously the five eagles took to noisy flight. The great cat promptly withdrew into cover again, and did not re-emerge until dusk was so deep that photography had become impossible.

A pair of Tawny Eagles will often lay their eggs year after year on the same stick nest skied in a tree, adding fresh building twigs and leafy cushioning to it every twelve months, until it becomes quite a vast edifice. In it they hatch usually one, but sometimes two chicks.

* *The Mystery of the Flamingo*, by Leslie Brown.

Eland

Taurotragus oryx

The eland is the largest and heaviest of all East African antelopes. Massively cattle-like in build, an adult bull stands about six feet tall at the top of its humped shoulders, stretches some eleven feet long from snout to tail-base, and turns the scales at approximately 2,000 lbs. Although its movements are therefore necessarily less acrobatic than those of friskier, smaller antelopes, it can nevertheless be surprisingly lithe and energetic for so ponderous a beast. Its normal pace is a walk, which increases to a trot when stimulated by slight concern, and which accelerates into a gallop when provoked by true alarm—though that speed is maintained only over short distances. An excited, retreating heavyweight bull has been known to clear an eight-foot-tall fence at one leap; and I have watched an agitated herd careering forward with successive high jumps into the air, like a field of odd-looking steeplechasers racing in the Grand National. Some have been reported as skipping clean over a comrade's back. As for mountain climbing, elands (like elephants) have been recorded at 16,000 feet up the slopes of Mount Kilimanjaro.

Principally browsers on various leaves, pods and fruits growing in shrubs and trees, elands are inoffensive giants. Their horns, however, can be tough and grim, as I know from personal experience. Once upon a time I entered the enclosure of some allegedly tame elands at David Roberts' house on the shores of Lake Baringo, where he maintains a remarkable menagerie of beasts and birds for despatch to various of the world's Zoological Gardens. As I walked through the gate one of the elands advanced to greet me. It nuzzled me with its nose, and then bent its head and pinned me between its two horns against a wire-netting fence. I could not escape. When it twisted its head, and put pressure on my torso as if it were about to wrench me in two halves, I thought that Mr. Astley Maberly's tribute* declaring that 'Eland are remarkably gentle and inoffensive, and I do not think that even a wounded one has been known to charge' was perhaps about to be disproved. But I was wrong, and he was right. After a few not very gentle digs in the ribs, the beast gave me a friendly, satisfied glance, and turned and strolled away. Apparently its demonstration was just a neighbourly welcome!

Elands usually travel in small herds of between half-a-dozen and two dozen beasts; but when they migrate they form larger parties, occasionally numbering as many as two hundred animals. I have seen a group of sixty on the trek, and they made a splendid caravan as they meandered across beautiful wild country in Masailand.

* In *Animals of East Africa*, by C. T. Astley Maberly.

Elephant

Loxodonta africana

The present-day African and Asian elephants are the sole remaining descendants of a variegated assortment of pre-historic ancestors who roamed most parts of the world. That tribe had as many as 352 different branches; and the earliest surviving traces of their original Adam and Eve are elephantine fossils found in Egypt which date back some 50,000,000 years. Among subsequent offsprings of the order were the mastodons of Africa, Europe and America, the woolly mammoths of Siberia, the straight-tusked elephants of interglacial Europe, and the dwarf species of Sicily.

Today's African and Asian types differ from each other considerably in physique, temperament and capacities. The African beast is bigger (being the largest living animal on land) with a flatter skull and vaster ears; and it is also wilder, probably less amenable to discipline, and perhaps less intelligent than its Asian relative.

In other ways the two species are similar. That appears to be true of their love-life, which has charming touches of romance. When a bull and a cow elephant in a herd become attracted to each other, they start walking out together almost like a young human couple contemplating betrothal. Later they engage in flirtations such as fondling each other innocently with their trunks; and when the female's season arrives she engages in suggestive little acts to stimulate her partner's desire. As soon as she next comes on heat he falls violently in love with her. The pair keep company all day, mating two or three times at intervals of a few hours; and at dusk they slip away again together to continue their love-making. Authorities declare that their honeymoon may sometimes last several months, with elements of mutual solicitude in their relationship which indicate true affection.

In due course the female becomes pregnant, and gradually after that her inclinations turn from the pleasures of love to the more domestic responsibilities of motherhood. The couple separates; and some twenty months after its conception a baby elephant is born. It stays in its mother's care for several years, during which time she will mate with a new bull and produce a fresh calf about every three years.

I once had personal experience of the passion of an elephant in love. My wife Audrey and I were riding on a bull elephant through the Malayan jungle. The beast was enamoured of a cow elephant marching three individuals ahead of us in our Indian file procession through the dense forest; and he kept trying to break from our position to join her. But the path was too narrow to permit that; so he heaved, pranced and trumpeted with emotion as we advanced, and our howdah rocked like a small boat on a rough sea. He was love-sick, Audrey felt air-sick, and I was just plain sick.

The elephant pictured on the opposite page is an inhabitant of Amboseli Park; and behind it rises the snow-capped peak of Mount Kilimanjaro.

114

Lesser Flamingo

Phoeniconaias minor

The series of alkaline lakes along the floor of the Great Rift Valley in Kenya and Tanzania is the greatest assembly ground for flamingos in the world. East Africa's particular speciality is the Lesser Flamingo, of which some 3,000,000 may inhabit the area, whilst much smaller populations of the species spill over as far east as India and as far south as the Cape of Good Hope. Several tens of thousands of Greater Flamingos also reside along the East African portion of the Rift Valley.

They all prefer slightly saline lakes like those at Nakuru, Magadi and Natron to freshwater lakes like that at Naivasha, because their food consists of microscopic organisms such as algae which are more concentrated in the former. Often one can see several hundreds of thousands—and occasionally as many as two million—of the birds wading together in close-packed mobs, marching and counter-marching on their tall stilts as they bend their elegant necks and sweep their Roman-nosed beaks to and fro in the shallows. They fill their mouths with liquid, expel the pure water through filters with which their bills are equipped, and swallow the remaining mass of the soft substances which keep flamingos hale and hearty.

Some mystery surrounds their breeding seasons, which seem to be spasmodic and intermittent, sometimes with a break of years between one successful mating period and the next. That may be partly due to the vagaries of a climate in which droughts and floods are apt to occur erratically; for flamingos' fruitful nesting depends on the level of a lake being exactly convenient for the type of colonies they build. Each pair erects a pile of mud rather like a small ant-hill, and deposits two eggs in a dip on its summit. Hundreds of thousands of these edifices may arise in a multitude together, somewhat reminiscent of a small-scale model of a human city. An incubating flamingo sits astride every cone. To me all their resultant chicks look exactly alike; but each is recognisable to its parents, for they pick it out at once when they bring the youngster food. The same instantaneous recognition by parents of their own particular offspring among a seething throng of apparently identical chicks is characteristic of penguins, gannets, terns and other sea-birds which nest in vast colonies.

Two million flamingos gathered together is an awe-inspiring sight. When a multitude of individual birds raise their fluttering feathers on top of their lanky legs in territorial display, they have fantastic beauty. Leslie Brown's description of them as looking like 'huge pink feather dusters' is very apt, although perhaps Salim Ali's poetic phrase that they are 'like gigantic chrysanthemums' is even more appropriate, since there is always a touch of poesy about these fabulously majestic birds.

Bat-eared Fox

Otocyon megalotis

This charming little fox is a nocturnal hunter; but sometimes when its cubs are adolescent a family party will lie sleeping in daylight near the entrance of an underground burrow where the youngsters were born, and at that season they are visible to trippers in most of Kenya's National Parks and Game Reserves. We came across the group illustrated here dozing snugly among low scrub on Amboseli's sandy plain. At our approach the quintet rose reluctantly and trotted slowly away, looking back at us every now and then with uncertain curiosity rather than convinced suspicion. Before long they settled down again beside a small bush, and started to snooze once more. When we followed them they waited until we were quite near, and then rose and recommenced their half-hearted retreat. This act by us and them was repeated several times, until after some twenty minutes they began to grow accustomed to our land-rover, felt reassured that neither it nor we staring from its windows intended them any harm, and lay doggo even when we drove and stopped within ten yards of them.

Quite a strong breeze was blowing, and all five foxes huddled close together in the lee of a small protecting shrub, with their heads tucked low, their large bat-like ears collapsed in order not to catch the wind, and their tails wrapped tightly like blankets round their bodies. Their uncertainty about us was not entirely dissipated, however, for whilst four of them closed their eyes in sleep the fifth kept a watchful eye half-cocked in our direction—performing sentinel duty in case of treachery on our part.

After we finally withdrew, it, too, perhaps felt free to slumber; and probably they all stayed in the land of nod there much of the day. Towards dusk they would awake, uncurl themselves, and start their nightly foraging. Bat-eared Foxes have too weak teeth to tackle large prey, and are principally insectivorous; but they also enjoy small rodents like mice, lizards, the eggs and chicks of ground-nesting birds, some wild fruits, and tuberous roots. In their turn, they sometimes fall victims to the larger birds of prey. So for the preservation of their attractive species against the assaults of eagles as well as of Father Time, mating pairs resort periodically to subterranean lairs in sandy soil, where they produce litters of between three and five cubs.

This engaging animal's vital statistics are: length of body about two feet, length of tail one foot, and weight six to eight-and-a-half pounds.

Grant's Gazelle

Gazella granti

The most numerous animals on East Africa's wide plains and hills are various types of antelopes. They teem there in countless scores of thousands. Africa boasts between sixty-five and seventy-five different species of antelopes, their exact number being at present debatable, since the specific or sub-specific status of certain forms is still a subject of dispute among experts. The largest individual in the tribe is the Eland, and the smallest are Dik-diks and Pigmy Antelopes. In southern Kenya the commonest are those three lovely medium-sized creatures, the Impala, the Grant's Gazelle, and the Thomson's Gazelle.

The gazelles acquired their names from two of Africa's most intrepid explorers in the nineteenth century. Grant's Gazelle is larger than Thomson's. Its ram sports the biggest horns in relation to the proportion of the rest of its body of any animal in Africa; and their weight no doubt contributes to the erect, dignified mien with which the handsome beast holds itself.

These gazelles are regarded as rather small fry by lions, which usually hunt bigger game like wildebeests and zebras. But Grant's and Thomson's Gazelles are both favourite prey of cheetahs and wild dogs, who give them merciless chase. As I have already described, although the gazelles have a pretty turn of speed—being capable of maintaining forty-five miles per hour over long distances—their pursuers run them down.

Otherwise the innumerable herds of Grant's and Thomson's Gazelles have few enemies —except during the calving season. Then hyenas become their deadly foes, attended by jackals and vultures. When a ewe is about to produce her calf she leaves her herd for a short while to lie down and give birth. Ever-watchful hyenas know all the signs of such impending events, and lurk around ready to gobble the helpless youngsters as soon as they leave their mothers' wombs. However careful the ewes may be to conceal their new-born fawns in long grass, an appalling number of them suffer that fate. But the hyenas have to act quickly, because within an hour a tiny calf can rise and accompany its parent back to her herd's protection. Another helpful circumstance is the fact that large numbers of mother gazelles produce their calves at about the same time, with the result that however alert the hyenas may be, they find it impossible to murder the total new generation. That seems to be one of Nature's deliberate provisions by which, with cool impartiality between predators and their victims, it meets the needs of both alike.

Unlike thirsty Thomson's Gazelles, Grant's Gazelles appear capable of going without drink for months on end; and so they can exist in far more arid regions than their cousins. It is pleasing to come across a sudden lively party of them in barren-looking lands.

Thomson's Gazelle

Gazella thomsoni

Each species of African antelope has its own peculiar charm of form, movement and habits; but none for me excels in pretty grace the Thomson's Gazelle, or 'Tommy'.

One of the commonest and most numerous animals to be seen on Kenya's southern plains, it often gathers in very large herds. Sometimes a Tommy is tame and confiding, allowing you to approach quite close; but at other times it is shy and nervous, racing away as soon as you come within hailing distance. Smaller than most related species—its height at the shoulders being only two feet—it is lovely in figure, picturesque in colouring, neat in movement, and capable of an impressive turn of speed. When alarmed it sometimes resorts to a curious gait known as 'stotting'. Raising its head and tail erect, and—after a preliminary step or two—holding its four legs stiffly taut, it starts a succession of rigidly bouncing leaps which carry it forward swiftly as it gathers momentum. 'A kind of pogo-stick motion', writes Alan Moorehead of it in one of his sensitive, brilliant descriptions of Africa's wild game in his book *No Room in the Ark*; and on their pogo-sticks a whole herd of Tommies will skip hurriedly out of sight.

I am told that ewes adopt this action when trying to lure a hyena or jackal away from the lair of a new-born youngster. As in the case of Grant's Gazelles, expectant Tommy mothers leave their herds when about to give birth; and when a fawn is dropped the ewe grazes round it as it lies concealed in long grass. Usually only one youngster is born, but twins have sometimes been recorded. After a short while the fawn or fawns bestir themselves into active life, and within a few hours they are able to keep pace with their mothers as they wander back towards their herds.

The normal family group in a breeding season is a ram with his harem of several ewes accompanied by their offspring. As the young rams grow adolescent their presence becomes intolerable to their father, who wishes no rivals for his wives' favours. Often you come across little bachelor parties of such Tommy youths expelled from their parental groups. As they grow lusty they begin to feel the urge to look around for mates of their own, and in due time many a pitched battle is fought for possession of harems between those young aspiring males and veteran sires who are beginning to fail in strength. No doubt in instinctive training for such duels a couple of young bucks will often engage in playful sparring together, lowering their heads, locking their horns, and jabbing and thrusting at each other in mock attempts to gain a resounding victory.

As a result of such rivalries, during the mating season there is never a dull moment in the polygamous herds of gazelles and impalas. I shall write in greater detail about that domestic life in my note about the latter graceful animal.

Gerenuk

Litocranius walleri

All the antelopes have charm of appearance and movement; and among them the gerenuk is no exception. At the same time it has its own unique touch of grotesqueness. Graceful and lanky-legged, with a body about the size of an Impala's, it is distinguished by an unusually long, rather giraffe-like neck and head. Indeed, sometimes it is named the 'giraffe-gazelle', and that description—if scientifically nonsensical—is especially apt in the case of young rams whose horns have not yet far developed. Female gerenuks have no horns at all; but those of adult males are stout and nicely curved, although rather short compared with the lanky pairs on some other antelopes.

Like giraffes, gerenuks are browsers, eating no grass, but feeding on a myriad leaves, twigs and berries growing in the bush country which they inhabit. Like giraffes, too, they seem particularly fond of tender shoots sprouting near the tops of certain thorn trees. But unlike giraffes, although their necks are long enough to reach fairly high, gerenuks are not sufficiently tall when standing earthbound on four feet to grasp the most succulent tit-bits near the trees' summits. To reach those a gerenuk therefore raises itself airily on its hind-legs, stretches its body and neck to their full lengths and with most graceful balance nibbles at the lofty foliage. It can maintain that upright poise for considerable periods, helping to keep itself steady by dainty holds of its fore-hooves on branches. Some competent observers allege that they have seen a gerenuk increase its stretch an extra fraction of an inch by rising on tip-toe to bite a little higher—an unprecedented achievement among antelopes.

The series of pictures on the next page illustrates that attractive feeding act. I have already described in my introductory notes the surprising circumstances in which they were taken. They depict a youthful ram gerenuk with horns not yet fully grown. As we sat in our land-rover watching him he suddenly rose on his hind-legs, balanced himself with his fore-hooves against the branches of a tree, and started feeding on its high leaves. The four photographs display successive incidents in his subsequent actions. In the first he is still greedily chewing tender shoots growing near the tree-top; in the second he has finished all those morsels in the immediate vicinity, and is on the point of turning to shift his position; in the third he has caught sight of our land-rover as he turned, and remains delicately balanced on his hind-legs like a performing ballerina, staring inquisitively at us; and in the fourth he has decided to descend to firm earth, and stands four-footed on the ground as he contemplates us with slight suspicion. Perhaps the faint, and to him strange, sounds of Chris's camera as it took photographs of him had reached his ears; and his glance suggests that he is not at all sure whether he approves of her attempt to immortalise him in her set of pictures. But before long he became acquiescent, for he and a companion soon resumed their unconcerned feeding among bushes all around us.

124

Gerenuks are often shy creatures, trotting briskly into concealment amidst thick shrubberies at the appearance of a stranger. At other times their well-developed sense of curiosity
gets the better of them, and they will stand for quite a while motionless and rigid, staring
at some unaccustomed arrival. Then perhaps they become reassured, and recommence
leisurely browsing. Their movements are nimble, and their long necks and delicate heads
give them a look of slightly fantastic dignity. They are usually seen singly or in small
parties of only three, four, or a few more. Unlike their impala and gazelle relatives, ram
gerenuks do not indulge in a prolific multiplicity of wives. Sometimes they seem to be
monogamous; perhaps more normally they possess two or three spouses; but they never
keep large harems. The most engaging family parties are those in which a miniature
youngster trots gaily through the bushes alongside its parents.

Gerenuks seem to need little liquid refreshment in the form of drinking water, for they
seldom slake their thirsts at pools. Presumably they get all the sustenance of that nature
which they require from fluids in the fruits and leaves that they swallow. On the other hand,
a few of these antelopes who have been for several years inmates of Frankfurt Zoo are
quite often observed sipping each other's urine. Pundits suggest that this habit may be
common among them in the wilds, and that it is an adaption to the scarcity of water in
their normal habitat.

Gerenuks were known to the ancient Egyptians several thousand years ago, for their
carved figures appear on works of art dating back to the earliest dynasties along the Nile.
Then for some reason the creature passed completely out of mankind's artistic, literary and
scientific records, until it was rediscovered on the Somali coast towards the end of the
nineteenth century. Let us hope that this gracious animal will never get lost again.

Masai Giraffe

Giraffa camelopardalis

Two distinct types of giraffes exist in Kenya, the Masai Giraffe in the southern and central parts of the country, and the Reticulated Giraffe further north. They are similar except for the different markings on their coats. And they are unique in the animal kingdom. A male giraffe stands about 18 feet high from the soles of its hooves to the tips of its 'horns' (which are not real horns, but projections of bone covered with hairy skin), whilst the female grows to about 15 feet. A bull weighs approximately one ton.

Giraffes are browsing animals especially equipped with towering necks to enable them to feed on the high-growing foliage of acacia trees which is their favourite foodstuff. Through field-glasses one can watch their long, narrow tongues curl round, grasp and break off the desired shoots, with an action like that of a miniature elephant's trunk. Usually a giraffe's movements as it travels and feeds are leisurely, for it is a gentle, unaggressive creature. This natural trait is reflected in its large, long-lashed, beautiful eyes, which stare wistfully at you like the gaze of some pensive movie-starlette. Yet when provoked the animal can defend itself—also like a movie-star—with a vicious chop from one of its forelegs, or a sledge-hammer kick from a hind-leg, which can be fatal to any attacking man or beast. Such blows have been deadly for many a lion, which is the only serious enemy of giraffes.

If alarmed, a giraffe will turn tail and run away; but even then its gait has a leisurely air in keeping with its non-violent character. Moving its legs in pairs on either side, first the right hooves forward and then the left, with the hind-limbs reaching well in front of the fore-limbs at every stride, it progresses at an easy, undulating, slow-motion gallop as graceful as the movements of a racehorse slowing down after a classic sprint. Only when chased by a lion does it deign to accelerate into swift, energetic, full-tilt retreat.

Giraffes have been more generously equipped by Nature for 'necking' than any other animals on earth; and this activity does in fact play a part in their courtship. A male and a female will face each other, and join their necks in a series of caressing movements which make their heads bob and sway rhythmically. The necks slither up and down against one another, and writhe and intertwine in a constant succession of snaky movements. One strange fact about these necking bouts is that they occur at least as often between pairs of bulls as between members of the two sexes; and a photograph opposite illustrates such a homosexual display. Possibly the action in those cases is a kind of formal combat.

A mother giraffe sometimes produces twins. After their birth the family stays together for months, the youngsters appearing exact replicas in miniature of their elders. There is no more charming sight in all Nature than such a quartet ambling and browsing leisurely through wild bushland.

Reticulated Giraffe

Giraffa reticulata

As I have already written, Masai Giraffes and Reticulated Giraffes are very similar; and only in the colour and pattern of their coats do they markedly differ. That difference is well illustrated in the photographs of the two types in this book. Otherwise they are alike in anatomical make-up, natural character and habits; and I am told that most taxonomists now regard them as conspecific.

But they reside in different parts of Kenya. The Masai Giraffes on the previous page were photographed at Amboseli in Masailand whilst the Reticulated Giraffe was snapped much further north, beside the Uaso Nyiro river in the Samburu country. There, and in neighbouring regions, that giraffe is quite common—but the Masai giraffe is non-existent. In the same way the Reticulated specimen never appears further south.

A somewhat similar state of affairs exists in the cases of several other species of animals. For example, the Masai Ostrich in southern and central Kenya is alike in form, character and habits to the Somali Ostrich found in the north, yet the two are sufficiently different in colours and textures to be separate sub-species. So also different types of zebras, hartebeests, waterbucks and other beasts inhabit different areas of Kenya, although sometimes their haunts to some extent overlap.

No landscapes in Kenya are more beautiful than those in the homeland of the Reticulated Giraffe. Not far from the vast, flat semi-desert of the old Northern Frontier Province, their spaciousness seems boundless; yet the prospect there is not flat. Outcrops of mountains rise suddenly from the plains, often as solitary heights and at other times in brief ranges, the loftiest of them soaring more than 8,000 feet towards the sky. Of various shapes and sizes, here they are smooth and grass-grown, and there they are jagged, precipitous and rock-strewn. Along the meandering Uaso Nyiro river a forest of thick trees grows; but elsewhere such arbours are few, and even single trees are comparatively rare. A bushy scrub covers much of the land, and among it nestle the thatch-roofed manyattas of Samburu tribesmen.

Their herds of cattle are increasing steadily in numbers, and were in danger of grazing the country so bare that not only the vegetation suffered, but also the populations of elephants, lions, giraffes and other beautiful creatures around were threatened with extinction. Now the sensible Samburu chiefs and people have agreed that such destruction would be unfortunate, and indeed contrary to their own best interests, since they could be part-gainers if their territory became a profitable resort for tourists. So they have decided to withdraw their cattle from a certain area, which shall remain a Game Reserve where gracious creatures like the Reticulated Giraffe can continue to live and prosper.

Egyptian Goose

Alopochen aegyptiacus

From Egypt and the Sahara all the way south to the Cape of Good Hope this goose is a common resident. In Kenya it can be found almost wherever fresh water exists; and it abounds especially beside the lakes along the Great Rift Valley. Sometimes the birds move about in pairs, sometimes in small parties, and at other times in huge flocks. Possibly one reason for their apparently unrestricted multitude is that they make poor table food—at times almost uneatable. So they are not harried for the pot. That no doubt helps to explain also the comparatively unshy, confiding nature which they display. They have not learned to fear the two-legged creature called Man. Even when accompanied by a brood of young-sters, a hen will often show no undue concern at a human approach. Gathering them around her, she merely leads them away at an unhurried, dignified walk.

For the rearing of these goslings a pair's taste in nesting sites is catholic. Occasionally a hen lays her eggs in a short burrow underground; more frequently she deposits them on the earth's surface; and most often she skies them in an old, abandoned nest of some other large bird up a tree. Now and then a breeding couple takes temporary possession of some African villager's beehive slung beneath a bough; and other pairs have been known to breed in holes on rocky cliffs. In those various situations the geese construct a circle of grass and reeds well lined with soft down, and in it they incubate a clutch of between five and eight yellowish white eggs. In due course they coddle the same goodly number of downy youngsters.

That could raise a problem when the nest is lodged at some dizzy height. Numerous pairs of Egyptian Geese at Lake Naivasha, for example, rear their goslings in the disused nests of African Fish Eagles built in the tops of tall acacia trees along the shore. When the time arrives for the nestlings to come down to earth and water, how are they transported? Do their parents somehow convey them down, or do the youngsters take flying leaps into the air, trusting that they will land safe and sound in the strange world below? The answer seems to be the latter course. On the appointed day the young geese hurl themselves from their nests like suicides jumping from skyscraper windows—but with a result very different from the fate of those unhappy souls. Descending earthwards with outstretched wings and webbed feet acting like half-opened parachutes, they live to tell the tale in excited squawks when they eventually reach solid ground.

In later life they often perch in trees, where they usually roost at nights.

Great Crested Grebe
Podiceps cristatus

The handsome bird shown here was swimming on Lake Naivasha, and frequently a similarly beautiful companion swam close beside it. The month was June, and probably the pair owned a nest in the neighbourhood. But Great Crested Grebes are shy, wary birds who try to keep their nesting sites 'top secret'; and so the couple did their best to avoid our party as we boated on the lake. When grebes are alarmed they do not spread their wings and take to the air in hurried flight, but swim momentarily lower in the water, and then curve their graceful heads and necks forwards to submerge quietly into the depths below. In that manner this pair kept disappearing from our view; and we could never tell in which direction, or at what distance, they would reappear for a few moments to eye us again before sinking once more. Nor did we find their nest.

Like other species of grebes, Great Crested Grebes are birds with remarkable powers of submarine acrobatics, for they hunt almost all their food deep underwater. Sometimes they submerge silently and unobtrusively, causing scarcely a ripple on a pool's surface, as when they seek to escape the notice of a suspicious-looking stranger; and at other times they take a flying jump almost completely out of the water, turn a semi-somersault in mid-air, and plunge beneath the surface with a big splash like a man diving from a springboard. They do this particularly on a deep lake when they wish to summon momentum for a very extended immersion. Their food consists of fish, frogs and aquatic insects.

Their richly coloured, rather theatrical plumage has particular significance in the breeding season, when they exploit its every beautiful feature in some of the most spectacular courtship displays performed by any birds. The cock and the hen alike demonstrate to each other with fluffings of feathers, contortions of bodies, and ecstatic swimming movements reminiscent of a dramatic *pas de deux* in a ballet. The infatuated grebes are no doubt dancing their own interpretation of romantic passages in 'Swan Lake'.

At that period of their domestic affairs the pair are also busy constructing a floating nest made of dead water-weeds moored to reeds; and on it in due course the hen lays three or four eggs. When she leaves them for a while between long spells of incubation she usually conceals them from possible enemies by covering them with bits and pieces of plucked greenery, so that the construction seems like an accidental pile of vegetation.

Helmeted Guinea-fowl
Numida mitrata

Often in various parts of Kenya one comes across considerable flocks of these guinea-fowls strolling along a road, like a party of rather prim old dames taking an afternoon walk. The analogy is suggested by their mild-gazing eyes, skinny wrinkled faces, stiffly erect carriages, precise little steps, and black plumage covered all over with white dots conveying a hint of a respectable elderly Victorian spinster's dress. At the sight of an approaching land-rover, however, the bevy of birds immediately takes fright, and breaks into a panicky trot. After seeking in vain to escape along the open road stretching ahead, they turn aside in desperation, and break through the long grass bordering the track. Once protected from the highway by a few feet of vegetation, they recover their calm even though they remain in close, full view of the intruder; and they then halt and stare inquisitively back at the car.

Sometimes a flock includes as many as several scores of birds. These stroll around in a communal party, carefully inspecting, pecking and scratching at the ground, for they eat grubs, insects, roots, bulbs, seeds and other earthy substances. Every now and then one of the fowls disturbs their peaceful progress by making a sudden dart at another member of the group, and chasing it around in small circles. Whether this is a jealous male trying to punish a rival cock who has ventured too near his favourite hen, or a desirous male making a pass at a tempting female, or merely a hungry feeder shooing a trespasser from its own chosen pecking area, I do not know. Both sexes appear alike, and it is difficult to distinguish one from the other.

These and other guinea-fowls are related to pheasants and partridges; but they are sufficiently distinct in certain features to be easily recognisable. For example, they do not develop spurs on their heels, but use their beaks instead as weapons of offence and defence. Again, their skinny heads are naked except for a crest of feathers on some species, and a bony top-knot on others. The Helmeted Guinea-fowl's crown is a protrusion like a horn, reddish in colour, contrasting vividly with the pure blue wattles at the base of the bird's bill.

In the breeding season pairs leave their flocks and make nests in scratched-out hollows on the ground concealed among grass-tufts or low bushes, and lined with plucked grasses. Their hard-shelled, tough eggs number anything between half-a-dozen and twenty. When these yield up chicks after an incubation period lasting nearly a month, the parents and offspring continue to wander around in a family party whilst the youngsters learn how to feed and fend for themselves. Afterwards they all rejoin a flock.

Vulturine Guinea-fowl

Acryllium vulturinum

Among the five different species of guinea-fowls occurring in East Africa the Vulturine is easily distinguishable from the rest by its lack of any sort of head-crest. Of the other four, two sport a bony crest (like the Helmeted Guinea-fowl which I have just described), and two a feathery one.

In spite of its somewhat unprepossessing name, the Vulturine Guinea-fowl is a strikingly handsome bird with brilliant colouring and an elegant, long-tailed figure. Its upper mantle of lengthy feathers striped with white, black and cobalt-blue is a vivid flash of beauty, enhanced by its bare blue face and its scintillating blue breast feathers. The naked flesh of its head and neck, and the small size of that head in relation to the rest of its body, give it the name 'vulturine'.

Like other guinea-fowls, these are inclined to live in large, sociable flocks, except in the breeding season, when they separate into pairs. As soon as the new generation of fledgeling birds can fend for themselves many individual families re-unite in flocks once more. Sometimes different species of guinea-fowls join together in a common party. Towards evening at Uaso Nyiro, for example, I have come across a mixed flock of about a dozen Vulturine Guinea-fowls associating apparently indiscriminately with about a score of Helmeted Guinea-fowls. But as soon as I approached close they broke the partnership and went their separate ways, the Vulturines all spreading their wings and flying into low trees in one direction whilst the Helmeteds took to their heels and ran swiftly away in the opposite direction—almost as if they did not wish to be seen keeping company together.

Their association shows that to some extent different species of guinea-fowls frequent the same kind of country, although each seems to have its own distinct preference. The bony-crested birds are partial to open, forested and thorn-tree regions; the feather-crested ones prefer more densely thicketed and wooded valleys; and the Vulturine Guinea-fowls usually inhabit drier thorn-covered plains, semi-deserts and similar arid areas. These last-named birds appear capable of existing without water for an indefinite period, obtaining their moisture from bulbs and corms. Their plumage lends brilliant gleams of vivid colour to sometimes drab places.

Hammerkop

Scopus umbretta

The portrait opposite explains how the Hammerkop got its name. When the bird stands in repose on the ground, its large, thick beak protruding in front of its head, and its massive crest extending behind lend it the appearance of having a powerful hammer-head set on the handle of its neck. In this and other features both sexes are alike, except that the hen is usually somewhat smaller than the cock. The hammerkop's rather heron- or stork-like appearance is superficial, for the species is *sui generis*.

The birds usually stand singly or in pairs at a pond's or river's edge. They are almost invariably associated with water. That is because their favourite, though far from sole, food is frogs. When the breeding season approaches, a couple builds a gigantic nest in a tree beside a lake, pool or stream where later they can easily keep their chicks fed on plentiful tadpoles. As they wade through the water in search of their prey they deliberately shuffle their feet to stir up desirable meals.

Their nests are massive heaps of sticks like miniature haystacks lodged in the forks of trees. The countless twigs composing them are cunningly woven together round a burrow-like chamber in their midst. These nests can measure many feet in both height and width, and are probably the largest cradles for eggs and chicks built by any species of birds. That is surprising, since hammerkops are themselves only medium-sized creatures. It has been recorded that both birds of a pair working in energetic partnership every morning and evening took as long as four months to construct a nest; but usually the labour is less protracted. Nevertheless the cradle's size is so formidable that popular African belief in some regions declares that other kinds of birds assist in amassing the building materials. Instinctively the hammerkops always devise a small, round mud-lined entrance hole through the nest's thick wall on its most unapproachable side. Indoors they lodge anything from three to six eggs.

No other African bird is so much a subject of native legend. One widespread notion is that any person who molests a hammerkop will become a victim of ill fortune. No doubt as a result of this belief, the bird is comparatively free from human persecution; and probably that is why it often shows less concern than many other species at a human being's approach. I have often stood within a few feet of a hammerkop, admiring its charmingly grotesque figure, its rather imperturbable, tranquil nature, and its sagacious, wary and yet not unfriendly eye as it gazes serenely back at me.

African Marsh Harrier

Circus ranivorus

The European Marsh Harrier is a winter migrant to Africa, and it might be mistaken for the resident African species except that the latter is slightly smaller than the former, and also has certain distinguishing plumage markings. One of these is the barred tail- and wing-feathers revealed in flight, and shown in the upper photograph on the opposite page.

That picture of a hen at her nest was taken towards the end of June in the middle of marshy reed-beds at Kabete, a few miles from Nairobi. On the nest sat two fluffy, off-white, fiercely good-looking chicks beside one addled egg. They were only a few days old, and the parent harrier spent much of her time crouching protectively over them. Not far from the reed-bed a path wound through a field, and several times whilst I hid watchfully near the nest people strolled along that track and suddenly started talking as they passed by. The abrupt sound always startled the mother bird, who took off hurriedly; and on every occasion in her hasty, careless departure she accidentally kicked one of the chicks over the nest-edge into the reeds below! The evicted youngster lay helpless there until the old harrier returned a few minutes later, picked it up deftly by the top of its head in her beak, and dropped it back into the nest.

At other times the adult bird went off hunting. She never flew far, but from a dozen feet up in the air quartered carefully all the ground within a radius of a hundred yards round her home. Every now and then she dropped with upstretched wings and extended talons into the grass, and immediately afterwards I saw her tearing with her beak at some prey clutched in her feet. The fare could have been frogs, rats, mice, or small marsh birds. One of a harrier's favourite dishes is the little pink whistling tree-frog which frequents swampy areas near Nairobi—and which incidentally entertained my guests at Government House with nightly concerts of loud whistles in a courtyard surrounding a goldfish pool. Marsh harriers will also attack crippled ducks, but not unhurt ones; and whatever ducks may have been around that afternoon at Kabete must have been hale and hearty, for I observed no victim so large. Usually the huntress ate her catches herself on the spot where she caught them; but once she carried a small bird as food to the youngsters in the nest. They ravenously swallowed its torn-up bits and pieces.

Whilst the harrier in the upper photograph opposite is the hen at that nest, the handsome creature in the lower picture is a streak-breasted cock dallying in Nairobi's National Park.

Hartebeest

Alcelaphus buselaphus

Once upon a time hartebeests were among the most plentiful antelopes to be seen anywhere on Kenya's plains; but now they have become comparatively restricted in numbers and range. They usually associate in small herds, and are very alert, appointing one member of their group to act as a sentinel whilst the others graze. At the sight of danger that guardian utters a sharp snort—and away the whole company careers. Hartebeests can move very fast when they want to.

They are rather odd-looking creatures, with ears protruding like a second pair of horns above their unusually long faces, high withers, and steeply sloping hindquarters. Very sociable, they mix freely with wildebeests, zebras and ostriches, as well as with other antelopes. Such varied companies constitute an excellent mutual protection society, for certain of the species excel in their sense of hearing whilst others are more proficient in sight and yet others in smell. So between them they possess a very effective, comprehensive warning system against the approach of enemies.

Like some of those companion animals, hartebeests are much preyed upon by lions; and African Hunting Dogs are other terrible enemies. But European and African hunting men are their greatest foes, being the chief perpetrators of the indiscriminate slaughters which have so greatly reduced their numbers. A pair of handsome, spiralling hartebeest's horns adorn many a self-satisfied sportsman's walls.

The various sub-species of the breed of hartebeest found in Kenya include the Coke's, the Jackson's, and the Lelwel's. The animal commonly called Hunter's Hartebeest is not a true member of the family. It is included by C. A. W. Guggisberg* and other authorities among the 'bastard hartebeests', and is in fact a distant cousin of hartebeests who are not bastards. It has become famous because it is particularly scarce, being found until recently only in the Tana River area of north-eastern Kenya and in neighbouring Somalia. Not poachers alone, but also agricultural development, threaten it there; and so now, in an attempt to save the species, numbers of specimens are being transported to National Parks and Game Reserves where they will be fully protected. But they are not yet off the danger list.

In the picture opposite a Coke's Hartebeest is keeping company with a Grey-bearded Wildebeest, or Gnu. I shall write later about that darker, more solemn-looking neighbour.

* *Game Animals of Eastern Africa*, by C. A. W. Guggisberg.

Black-headed Heron

Ardea melanocephala

Every day of the year Black-headed Herons fly with slow, stately wing-beats above my garden. They are probably members of a nesting colony which first became resident in 1954 on a group of eucalyptus trees near Nairobi's railway station. In spite of the engines and trucks shunting just below them, the birds have occupied that site ever since; and Myles North joined them for long sessions of observation from the top of an eighty-foot-high tower at various times between 1958 and 1962. He gathered the following information.*

The colony of many scores of nests contains no other species than Black-headed Herons, although large numbers of Kites and Pied Crows use the same trees for roosting. The other principal intruder is an African Hawk-eagle which occasionally visits the place to help itself to a young heron on a nest. At such acts of aggression the parent birds and their neighbours fly around uttering agitated protests, but never plucking up courage to descend and drive the murderer away.

Breeding in the colony continues all through the twelve months, and has done so without cease year after year. A similar state of affairs has been reported from a Black-headed Heron's colony at Kampala during the last twenty years. This practice may be an exception rather than the rule for these herons, since evidence from other places suggests that their nesting is usually seasonal rather than non-stop. An interesting detail is that the eyes of breeding birds change colour from yellow to red.

Although breeding in the Nairobi heronry is continuous, there are distinct peaks in nesting activity at the rainy seasons, and comparative lulls during the dry spells. The breeding cycle of a pair lasts some 100 days, consisting of approximately 15 days for courtship and nest-building, 25 days for incubation of eggs, and 60 days for the care of the young. Both parents share in all those duties, with constant noisy comings and goings by the adult population. The elders feed their offspring by regurgitation, on rodents, grasshoppers, fish, beetles, birds, vegetable matter, frogs, crabs and other delicacies.

After about six weeks on their nests the fledgelings fly. At first, with awkward gestures, they wing their way from their cradles to near-by branches on surrounding trees. But they still depend on their parents for food, and those adults never feed them anywhere except on the nests; so the youngsters keep returning home for nourishment. That final stage of their youth lasts about a fortnight, after which they leave the colony.

Elsewhere in Kenya many Black-headed Herons do not breed in colonies confined to their own kind, but mix in settlements of various other nesting birds like cormorants, ibises and spoonbills. The immature bird pictured opposite had recently flown from such a community at Amboseli.

* *Breeding of the Blackheaded Heron at Nairobi*, by M. E. W. North (reprinted from The Journal of the East Africa Natural History Society and Coryndon Museum).

Buff-backed Heron, or Cattle Egret

Bubulcus ibis

Some interesting regular associations exist between particular species of African wild beasts and birds. A notable example is the partnership between the rhinoceros and the ox-pecker. Many a hefty rhino is accompanied wherever it goes by two or three of those starling-sized birds sitting on its back, hopping all over its body, and strolling across its face, where they invade its ears, nostrils and eyelids as they feed on innumerable ticks and blood-sucking flies which reside on the wrinkled skin or open sores. Nor do ox-peckers thus minister only to rhinoceroses, for they perform a similar service for elephants, elands and other large game, as well as for domestic cattle. It is said that the big game receive an additional reward for their tolerance of this parasitic occupation of their persons, since the sharp-eyed ox-peckers observe the approach of danger long before short-sighted beasts like rhinoceroses and elephants do; and they promptly give an alarm. Many a big-game hunter stalking such prizes has cursed the birds as they sighted him from afar, shuffled on to the backs of their patrons, and hissed a warning note—whereat the rhinos or jumbos beat a hasty retreat.

Another interesting association is that of Buff-backed Herons, or Cattle Egrets, with elephants, wildebeests and other heavyweight grazers. Again, the birds' purpose is gastronomic. They consume large numbers of grasshoppers, beetles and other flying insects which abound on grassy plains; and little flocks of the egrets therefore accompany grazing herds of game wherever they stroll through the pasture kicking up droves of those insects as they advance. One of the birds' favourite aides is the elephant, for naturally that giant's heavy feet are most disturbing to the desired grasshoppers, beetles and other victims. Half-a-dozen egrets may be seen wandering round an elephant's feet, apparently in great danger of being crushed by its ambling gait, but always quick to evade the heavy footfalls whilst at the same time capturing their tiny prey. Frequently, when the birds' greed is satisfied for a while, they fly aloft on to the elephants' backs, and ride there like Maharajahs —until pangs of hunger accost them again, and they descend once more to pursue their sport around the elephants' legs.

Their similar exploitation of domestic cattle gained them long ago their best-known name of Cattle Egret. Incidentally, they are almost omnivorous of large insects, swallowing aquatic species as readily as land-lubbers. And since birds cannot live by bread alone, but must periodically resort to love-making to ensure the survival of their species, these egrets at that crisis in their lives build nests in colonies near water, where they are surrounded by easily available, endless meals.

Goliath Heron

Ardea goliath

The largest of numerous African herons, a full-grown Goliath Heron stands about five feet tall. Its food consists wholly of fish and similar aquatic creatures; and so it spends most of its time angling.

I have often watched a bird engaged in that sport. It will stand completely motionless knee-deep in water for fifteen minutes, half an hour, an hour, or longer waiting with unbelievable patience for a minnow or an eel to swim by. If at the end of the vigil none has appeared, the heron betrays no hint of frustration, but lifts one foot extremely cautiously out of the water, stretches it very, very slowly forwards, and dips it with excruciating gradualness into the depths again, advancing one short step with such tedious, almost unmoving deliberation that not the tiniest, faintest quiver of a ripple disturbs the pool. All the time the bird's eyes are gazing keenly into the deep, and its beak is held like an unsheathed sword ready to strike. I have observed the painstaking fisherman spend a couple of hours within a few feet of the same spot without so much as catching a glimpse of a prey. It never seems to lose hope. Indeed, I am inclined to think that the patience of a Goliath Heron is even more inexhaustible than that of Job, and that it would be a higher compliment to be described as having 'the patience of a Goliath Heron' than as having the patience of the famous prophet.

Every year these birds nest in a colony on Gibraltar Island in the middle of Lake Baringo. About thirty pairs were breeding there when the photograph opposite was taken in mid-May. Some nests were perched on trees, others sprawled on bare stone promontories or shrubs protruding up the high cliff-face, and yet others lay marooned on rocks in the water below. Some contained a clutch of three or four eggs, others bore both eggs and chicks, and yet others housed a whole family of nestlings.

Both birds of a pair brought food to their youngsters. An adult would fly away and catch three or four fish, store them in its gullet, and then return to the nursery and spew them on to the nest floor. It had little discrimination as to the size of fish it should bring for any particular size of young heron. In the nest illustrated here, for example, a solitary tiny, day-old chick squatted beside an unhatched egg. A parent arrived and spat out two large fish. The chick took no notice of them, at which the adult swallowed them again, and flew away. Some time later it returned, and once more regurgitated the same brace of fish. The youngster appeared to suck rather than nibble at one of them with its inexperienced, inefficient bill; and the parent tried to help by pecking at the fish to break it into smaller pieces—but with little nutritive result so far as its offspring was concerned.

Hippopotamus

Hippopotamus amphibius

Often the only fragmentary glimpse that one catches of a Hippopotamus is its small ears, periscopic eyes, and flattish snout protruding an inch or two above the surface of a pool, like features on the face of some gigantic frog. The rest of its massive, two-tons-or-more figure is left to the imagination, sunk in water. At other times a group of the titans will wallow more exposed in their bath, as can frequently be seen at Mzima Springs in Tsavo Park. One day I watched a party of twenty hippos soaking by the hour there, most of the time completely submerged, but every now and then heaving their heads and backs above the surface like vast chunks of primitively sculptured rocks being catapulted upwards by an earthquake. They were so jumbled together that usually it was difficult to tell which ugly face belonged to which repulsive body. Every now and then one of them suddenly bellowed 'Hoosh! Haw-haw-haw-haw!', and its companions echoed the sentiment in a chorus of shattering grunts and snorts. The conversation piece on the opposite page is an impression of that gathering.

Usually hippopotamuses continue bathing all day long, and only emerge on to dry land at dusk to commence their nightly foraging for waterside plants. Generally they are rather peaceable, good-natured creatures; but sometimes fierce fights break out between rival bulls, in which the combatants inflict fearful wounds on each other with their sharp-edged lower-jaw tusks. One such duel is in progress in the picture on the next page. I watched the two beasts portrayed there tussling together below water, and periodically raising their heads above it to gasp fresh air without abandoning their struggle. They bit each other viciously, and one of them once grabbed the other's head in its wide-stretched mouth, and shook it as a dog might shake a rabbit. Occasionally such battles only end in death.

I observed other episodes in the domestic life of those Tsavo hippopotamuses. For instance, I spied a mother hippo suckling her baby beneath the crystal-clear water. She lay on her side in comparative shallows, entirely submerged, but in a position where she could protrude her nostrils periodically above the pool's surface to take in hefty gasps of fresh air—for the beasts must lift their snouts from the depths every few minutes to breathe. The youngster fed at her teats, also completely underwater; but at regular intervals it kicked itself off from the pool's floor, and shot to the surface to take in air. Then it sank again to its mother's milk supply.

A submarine observation tank has been constructed in the river below Mzima Springs, from which one can watch the life of fish, eels, diving water-fowl and other aquatic animals. I sat there for many hours learning about their fascinating underwater habits. I always hoped that a hippopotamus would pass that way, so that I should see the monster's light fantastic amble along the river-bed. I could hear some of the beasts snorting, blowing and grunting farther upstream. At last one of them wandered in my direction, swimming

right past my window. But it kicked up so much earthy muck as it advanced that a cloud of the stuff floated all around it, obscuring my view. I could see only a vague shadow of the giant as it strolled within ten yards of me, followed by two other similar ghostly figures. I caught a clear glimpse of their heads only when they re-surfaced for a breather a little farther downstream.

I realised that if they returned up-river, I might get an unobstructed view of them, since the mud which they kicked up would then float to their rear, because they would be progressing against a down-flowing current. So I waited hopefully. But they stayed gambolling, puffing and blowing for an inordinate time at a considerable distance below my look-out, and I had just finally reconciled myself to disappointment, and was rising to depart for a picnic lunch on the river bank above—when I saw one of the most extraordinary sights that I have ever seen. The apparition materialised with no warning, and for a fraction of a second I could scarcely believe my eyes. In the watery depths beyond my window a colossal mother hippopotamus passed within a few feet of me, half walking and half swimming upstream, and at her side a baby hippo hastened to keep pace with her. The sediment which they displaced flowed rapidly backwards from them, so I got a completely clear view of them both. Their eyes were wide open, evidently observing alertly every movement around them. Probably they caught sight of my astonished gesture as I sat down to gaze at them, for they quickened their pace and hurried forward more purposefully. The youngster in particular had the light, floating demeanour of a creature 'walking on air' as it partly strolled and partly swam beside its mama.

The enchanting, if almost elephantine, mother and child were not the only participants in their procession. Immediately behind them, almost on their tails, swam an eager escort of the fish which prey on grubs attached to hippopotamuses' thick hides. They manoeuvred hither and thither like a squadron of small fighter aircraft escorting a gigantic bomber and its smaller model on some deadly expedition.

Occasionally in daylight one catches sight of a hippopotamus on dry land. In such circumstances the monster is shy, embarrassed, and quickly retiring. Amiable by nature, its last thought is aggression, and its first thought is self-preservation. Like a modest, abashed—and deplorably obese—maiden surprised unexpectedly in the nude, it retreats swiftly from sight into thick reeds.

Hornbills

Twenty different species of these rather grotesque birds occur in East Africa. The massive bills of the Grey Hornbill on the opposite page, and of the Redbilled Hornbill overleaf, are modest, unassuming, almost self-effacing features compared with the beaks of some other species. The Trumpeter, Black-wattled, Silvery-cheeked, White-thighed, and Black-and-white Casqued Hornbills have gigantic, triple-decker bills which give those birds an unbelievably top-heavy and rather clownish appearance. Unfortunately only two or three of these other African types visit Kenya; and none of them ever came within shooting distance of Chris's camera.

Grey Hornbill
Tockus nasutus

The Grey Hornbill, as also the Redbilled, practises the strange habit of nesting adopted by most members of the tribe. The hen lays her eggs in a large hole inside a tree-trunk; she then sits tight on them whilst the nest entrance is almost completely closed by a dung wall raised by her mate and herself; she stays imprisoned there for many weeks, first incubating the eggs and then tending the chicks whilst the cock bird feeds her and them through a narrow slit in the wall; and only when her youngsters have grown quite large does she break out to assist the male in his duties as breadwinner. After her liberation they re-seal the nest wall so that the nestlings remain secure indoors for another two or three weeks, until they themselves are ready to fly. Presumably that wall is a protection for the eggs and chicks against tree-climbing enemies throughout those crucial months.

Redbilled Hornbill
Tockus erythrorhynchus

The illustration on the next page shows a Redbilled Hornbill flying from such a nest after feeding its offspring incarcerated within. The narrow perpendicular slit of the nest entrance appears on the tree-trunk just above the bird's tail. The youngsters were evidently growing lusty, for the hen had already ended her imprisonment with them, and had rejoined her mate outside.

I watched the family for the better part of three days. At first when Chris's hide was constructed six yards away the parents were nervous about visiting their nursery. Indeed, one of them flew into the tree four times with food for the nestlings gripped in its beak, fluttered from bough to bough making agitated little ejaculations, but never plucked up courage to go to the nest, and eventually swallowed the food itself each time, and flew away.

Later the adult birds overcame their nervousness, and resumed their normal parental activities. I observed them through most of each day from sunrise to sunset. The first parent would arrive with food for the youngsters within a few minutes of seven o'clock each morning, and except for a break in the middle of the day the pair would continue regular, frequent visits until half-past-six every evening, when (again at almost exactly the same moment by the clock each day) they went off duty for the night. When the first food-bringer arrived at dawn it was greeted by an enthusiastic clamour from the young birds, who were evidently feeling pangs of hunger after more than twelve hours abstinence. Their vocal reception was sometimes reiterated at later visits during the day, but in a more 'pianissimo' key as their sense of starvation receded.

The adults took turns to do a spell of feeding their dependants, each separate shift lasting between twenty minutes and half-an-hour. The current supplier would alight on the tree-trunk below the nest entrance, insert the tip of its bill (which was all that could penetrate) through the slit, and pass a morsel of food to one of the eager beaks indoors. Mostly the fare was grasshoppers and sometimes caterpillars, but occasionally a berry, beetle, lizard or praying mantis was provided instead. As soon as it had been delivered the bird turned tail, sped to a perch on a neighbouring branch, wiped both sides of its hefty bill on the bough, and then flew away to fetch another morsel. In the early part of the day these visits occurred about every four minutes for hours on end, but later the pace slackened somewhat to approximately once every seven minutes, with occasional rather longer interludes.

The youngsters hidden in the tree were admirably house-trained. Every now and then one of their beaks appeared at the nest entrance gripping a 'faecal sac' which it hurled into outer space. On other occasions when a nestling wished to relieve itself it propped its posterior against the entrance, and shot out a little squirt of excrement. So the nest itself remained unfouled throughout its months of occupation.

As I have said, the parents took turns at feeding their family. The one off duty spent the intervals feeding itself, storing up fresh energy for its next bout of service. It usually hunted along the ground, although occasionally it cocked an eye to a bush overhead in search of a berry. Proceeding by a series of single big hops across the grass, it kept turning over bits of wood, heaps of fallen leaves, or lumps of earth with the tip of its beak to inspect their undersides, or making sideways scrapes with the bill through the soil in attempts to contact prey. It caught quite a lot.

The nest-tree stood near a house where a barnyard contained some domestic cocks and hens which laid eggs for the householders. Sometimes a hornbill intruded into the yard, and started hunting there; but soon an irate hen would run at it and chase it away, undeterred by the invader's hefty, weaponlike beak. The hornbill never used that weapon, and docilely withdrew.

Spotted Hyena

Crocuta crocuta

I believe we are grossly unjust in our criticisms of hyenas. The trouble is that we are apt to draw analogies between animal behaviour and human behaviour, and to require that beasts should observe the moral code of conduct laid down for ourselves in civilised society. That is unfair, since the law of Nature is sometimes very different from the law of Man.

It is true that if a man prowled around at nights with a 'mean', 'hang-dog', 'guilty' look (all popular descriptions of a hyena's glance), emitting 'a repulsive smell', and devouring dead or dying animals, we should think his manners left something to be desired. Yet, incidentally, many men cannot plead innocent to a charge of not dissimilar behaviour. Often their favourite dishes are young birds or beasts which have been first artificially stuffed with food, then prematurely killed, and finally cunningly cooked, precisely for their gastronomic pleasure. And as for the human smell, occasionally quite charming people give off odours somewhat disturbing to their own fellows, and most of us possess a whiff which is intolerable to many other animals. I am told that the reason why water-buffaloes are apt to charge European visitors in the Far East is that the white man's smell—as distinct from that of the brown or yellow man—is utterly repulsive to the worthy creatures' sensitive nostrils.

As for the adjectives 'mean', 'guilty', and so on applied to the look in a hyena's eyes, these are anthropomorphic terms which probably have no application whatever to the feelings inspiring the beast's gaze. Such animals are certainly unaware of guilt, meanness or other regrettable qualities. Their stare is wary, suspicious, or fearful—as it often has every right to be.

I do not suggest that a hyena is a little angel, a paragon of all the virtues. It is not. It is just a mixture of strengths and weaknesses. Sometimes, for example, it shows abject cowardice, and at other times it displays remarkable courage. It is, for instance, the only scavenger whom such valiant hunters as leopards incline to fear. And above all, even if its taste is appalling—no rotting carcass being too filthy for its enjoyment—that predilection enables it to perform a most valuable service to all the other members of the animal kingdom, including human beings. By devouring putrid corpses it reduces greatly the risk of the spread of dangerous diseases.

Africa's Spotted Hyena is the largest and most powerful hyena on Earth. And it is splendidly equipped to perform its tasks, possessing the strongest jaws of any living mammal, with powerful teeth which permit it to crack the toughest bones.

Rock Hyrax

Heterohyrax brucei

A Rock Hyrax looks rather like a guinea-pig, and a full-grown specimen attains the size of a large rabbit without the rabbit's lanky ears. So it is quite a small animal. That makes its most distinguished characteristic all the more astonishing—for it is the nearest living relation of the elephant! The other closest surviving relative of that giant is the sea-cow, which haunts the waters of the Caribbean and other salubrious seas, but is not found off African shores.

Those surprising facts were established by anatomists who showed that the hyrax, the elephant and the sea-cow share certain common features absent in every other form of life. The most important of these concerns the bone structure of their feet. But even the most cold-blooded scientists could scarcely believe the correctness of their analysis until excavations in Upper Egypt revealed fossilised remains of similar ancestors of the elephants and the hyraxes who lived almost contemporaneously 50,000,000 years ago.

Today Rock Hyraxes—which are unique to Africa—reside chiefly in rocky boulders and cliffs, or among large outcrops in stony ravines. They are gregarious, associating in large parties amidst such haunts. Although they eat their vegetarian meals mostly at nights, they are abroad through much of the day, liking to bask in sunshine on rock terraces. If all the members of a group appear to be snoozing, nevertheless at least one of their number is in fact keeping a look-out for pythons in the undergrowth, leopards among the boulders, and eagles in the sky—the creatures which are their principal enemies. When alarmed the party runs quickly into hiding in crevices among the rocks; but as soon as they feel re-assured they creep out-of-doors again to continue their sun-baths. Their feet have rubbery soles which enable them to climb easily up sheer cliff faces.

They are plentiful in various parts of Kenya. The engaging sample portrayed here is squatting on a boulder which was a fragment in one of the most recent streams of lava spewed from a volcano in the Tsavo National Park. That eruption occurred about 500 years ago, and the lava is now a cold column of dead stones stretching across the vivid green bush. One of the attractions of Tsavo is its landscapes riddled with extinct volcanoes.

Another species of hyrax—and relation of the elephant—is the Tree Hyrax. A nocturnal feeder, its weird rattling midnight calls working up to a crescendo of high wailing have struck fear into the heart of many a suddenly woken traveller, convincing him that murder was being committed in the darkness close beside his bed.

Hadada Ibis

Hagedashia hagedash

This ibis is a fairly common resident throughout East Africa, and is usually found in the vicinity of lakes, swamps or rivers margined by trees. But it also frequents drier pasture lands. The specimen shown here was one of a pair in such a locality, for the two birds strolled around extracting worms and other large insects from the ground in front of the tourists' bandas at Amboseli. They were not unduly shy of human beings, tolerating with indifference the presence of the trippers who frequently stepped in and out of the near-by huts; and they showed only some suspicion, but no stronger objection, at being photographed in the open from twenty feet away. When Chris and her camera attempted to approach them closer they became a trifle concerned; but they merely took a short flight over a hedge into the game warden's garden next door, and continued their meal on the lawn beside his house. When she pursued them into that domestic pleasance they eyed her again with curiosity rather than alarm, until she approached cautiously, step by step, so near that they, with reciprocal caution, fluttered a few feet farther away. Perching on a pole in the garden fence from which they could get a more commanding view of her, and whence they could beat a hasty retreat if she advanced significantly closer, they eyed her uncertainly—but not unfriendlily. At that she halted, set up her camera on its tripod, and made all the necessary preparations with her lens and light-meter. The ibises stayed content, and for the next twenty minutes posed obligingly in various stances, which incidentally showed off to advantage their fine figures glistening with metallic purple and green on their backs and wings.

Most birds in Kenya's wilds seem distinctly less shy than those in similar places in Europe or America. They do not regard Mankind as an enemy, and continue to stand or stroll around in his (or her) near presence with comparatively little concern. The portrait gallery in this book demonstrates many instances of such fearless, neighbourly indifference.

Sacred Ibis

Threskiornis aethiopicus

In the days of the Pharaohs this ibis was a common resident of Egypt, where it was held in high respect. Its image appears on many paintings in royal tombs, and was a favourite model also for sculpture and other artistic forms. A subject even of worship, one of the gods wore an ibis's head; and the bird's present name is an echo of those ancient times. But now it is scarcely ever seen on the Lower Nile. Resident everywhere else on the vast African continent, it has for some reason almost abandoned its early Egyptian home.

An adult bird of either sex is mostly white with touches of iridescent green, except for a prominent patch of black at each of its two extremities. Its small head, long neck, and formidable down-curving beak are all pitch-black; and there is a group of purple-black plumes above its tail. The colour of its head and neck is not that of feathering, for no plumage grows there. It is the pigment of the bird's bare skin; and in that way the ibis appears a true African, as black as any Bantu son of the soil. Immature birds have different features, their heads and necks being covered with mottled black and white feathers.

The birds' most customary food is fish or frogs, although they also dig worms out of soft ground, and guzzle small reptiles, and insects such as locusts. So their favourite haunts are rivers, lakes and coastlines, where they hunt alone or in very small parties along the shores. Their appearance is rather solemn, and their step is sedate as they stroll or wade in search of prey.

In the breeding season Sacred Ibises become gregarious, nesting in colonies inhabited also by other water-loving birds. A considerable number of pairs then join the assembly at Lake Naivasha which I have already described. On the half-submerged trees in that avian suburbia they build large stick platforms with shallow depressions to hold their precious cargoes. Most of them bear three chalky white, rufous-splashed eggs, which in due course break into a trio of fluffy black and white chicks. Both adult ibises then do duty bringing food to the youngsters. At more or less regular intervals they go wading in the shallows, catch a nice kettle of fish which they store in their gullets, and return home to their offspring. Those instinctively knowing juveniles stick their small beaks far into their elders' long, open mandibles, tickle the parental throats to stimulate regurgitation, and so capture the treasure.

The bird posing on the opposite page is one of those parents so engaged. The protuberance of its throat shows that it is bringing a goodly ration of refreshments to a young family.

Impala

Aepyceros melampus

No doubt different people select different favourites among the numerous species of antelopes which frequent Kenya's wilds. Some regard the handsome Grant's Gazelle as the most attractive, and others choose the pretty Thomson's Gazelle; but probably a majority give the prize for all-in-all beauty to the Impala. Certainly it would be difficult to conceive an animal more graceful in combined form and movement than a running buck impala, with his slim, strong, leaping body, and his head crowned by splendid lyre-shaped horns. Although no one with good taste would criticise the doe's pleasing figure, she is less striking because she wears no horns. The portrait opposite shows a male impala, and the lower picture on the next page shows a party of females.

Being both browsers and grazers, these antelopes are more widespread and common than others, feeling at home in many kinds of country. But they are dependent on water for drinking, and so they do not stray into arid regions.

The most astonishing attainment of impalas is their power of jumping. They can combine a long jump and a high jump in a single spring; and they are the champion jumpers in Africa, far excelling even the famous springboks of South Africa. If suddenly startled, they will traverse a thirty-five-foot-wide road with ease at one flying leap which would also clear a ten-foot-high gate. In three consecutive strides an impala can cover more than seventy feet; and when chased by a lion the accomplished athlete has been known to elude capture by turning and leaping right over its pursuer. At other times impalas just jump for the sheer joy of jumping. A party of them will get into skittish mood, career round a confined space of ground in single file like animals on a merry-go-round, and as they come to a certain spot they will each in turn do a high jump, as if they were a team of competitors testing who can leap the highest.

In the non-breeding season they gather in various types of parties. Some are groups of adolescents of both sexes, others are 'stag' parties of mature bucks, and yet others are herds of does and their young with several bucks thrown in. But in the mating season such companies as the last are unthinkable to any self-respecting 'he' impala. The usual herd then consists of a solitary male with his ample harem of does. He is easily recognisable by his stately horns among his bevy of hornless beauties. Usually such a buck is the lord of a company of anything between ten and fifty wives; but sometimes his females are as few as half-a-dozen, and occasionally they count as many as a hundred. The more there are of them, the more he has his work cut out to preserve possession of the hoard. Intensely jealous, he keeps an eye on them all, every now and then circling round them, like a sheep-dog ensuring that a flock of sheep do not stray in undesirable directions. Unattached rival bucks are never far away, and some of the does are only too inclined to make more or less innocent eyes at them, to respond to an instinctive temptation to flirt with them, and to get

enticed away. When her lord and master sees one of them starting to do that he promptly chases her, and brings her back to the fold. And if a rival male throws down a gauntlet by venturing boldly near the herd, he at once attacks him. Usually the challenger runs away; but sometimes he intends his bid seriously, and stands to fight. Then a battle royal takes place. The combatants lower their heads with horns levelled threateningly at each other, as is shown in a picture opposite; and each tries to lock those formidable weapons against the other's in a grip which will force the enemy to capitulate and leave the field. Often those duels continue for a long time, and sometimes they end in death.

I heard such a fight taking place one early morning in Tsavo Park. It occurred about a quarter of a mile from a banda where I lay asleep in bed. Its fierce noises woke me; but unfortunately the duellists and their audience of does—for whose favour they fought—were hidden in a dip of ground beyond my view. The battle continued for twenty minutes, with frequent exclamations of mutual rage so loud that at first I thought the contestants must be much larger animals than impalas. A sort of roaring, snorting, growling and other passionate clashing constantly rent the air. Then a sudden deathly silence followed, and a few moments later the defeated buck cantered in retreat across the grass in front of my verandah. I never saw a more pathetically upset and agitated animal. As it withdrew it began snorting and growling again with violent sorrow, rage or humiliation; but it never looked back as it hastened out of sight.

Sometimes the established owner of a harem wins the battle, but at other times his challenger claims the victory. Then the latter takes possession of the wealth of female property at stake, whilst the vanquished beast retires regretfully to a life of monastic solitude. On yet other occasions the fight continues so long, and the harem boss is so preoccupied in waging it, that in his absence a second rival buck quietly steals upon his company of does, woos them—and makes off with the lot. The females always seem willing to switch their favours to whichever potent male beckons most strongly to them. Even if their recent lord then wins his duel, and chases the first challenger away, his triumph is hollow—for on turning to receive the congratulations of his wives he finds that they have all absconded with a new master!

At other times an aspiring young buck will manage to detach a portion of a harem belonging to an old male; and the bevy of consorts splits in two. So there is a fairly frequent splintering and reassorting of herds and their owners. Life for impalas is a constant adventure, with never a dull moment.

African Jacana

Actophilornis africanus

This jacana's popular name is 'Lily-trotter', and it spends most of its time being exactly that. Its featherweight body and long-toed feet enable it to alight on thin floors of water-lily pads floating on ponds and lakes, and to stroll across them at ease. The pastime is congenial to the bird, for it feeds entirely on aquatic molluscs and insects which attach themselves to the stalks and leaves of such plants. The fantastically, clownishly large feet which permit jacanas to balance and run on those flimsy foundations—like skaters on extremely thin ice—are notable examples of Nature's adaptation of an animal's physical features to its elemental needs. A sample of the feet is displayed in the portrait opposite.

At certain periods of each day the birds seem tireless in the performance of their balancing acts. Each individual or pair appears to have its own well-defined watery 'territory'. It shares the area in conspicuous mutual tolerance with such other species of water-edge birds as bitterns, moorhens and crakes—but it will not permit any intrusion by another jacana! If one does appear, the local landlord interrupts its feeding for a few moments to chase the trespasser helter-skelter out of sight.

Each 'territory' covers a comparatively small area; and it must be well-stocked with food. I have often watched, fascinated, an African Jacana engaged on a hunting safari. The bird strolls with quick, nimble steps across a stretch of lily-pads or other water plants, its body bent forward, and its neck stretched outward as its eyes search keenly for prey. With swift, darting movements of its beak it snatches a grub here, a snail there, or some other insect elsewhere. Every now and then it halts momentarily to turn some likely-looking leaf over for inspection of its underparts, sometimes tugging vigorously at an obstinately rooted weed which seems to be hiding treasure trove. When the bird has completed a thorough examination of a whole patch of greenery, it will hop, skip, jump or flutter to a neighbouring patch, and there repeat the performance all over again. And when it has finished the inspection of every successive patch within its territory, one after the other, it turns and retraces its steps back across the whole series of hunting grounds, repeating the process of search and grab at every stride. So it quarters over and over again the identical area of leafage covering a pool, rather like a policeman keeping a particularly sharp look-out for every significant detail as he walks to and fro along his beat.

Jacanas' nests are sodden platforms of water-weeds lightly moored near a lake's edge, where they sometimes get blown about in a breeze. So from their earliest hatched moments the chicks grow accustomed to a more or less sailing-boat existence.

Silver-backed Jackal
Canis mesomelas

I confess to a sneaking regard for the Silver-backed Jackal. No doubt its habits leave much to be desired if judged by impeccably correct standards of human conduct. It is usually a scavenger which contents itself with eating the left-over kills of nobler predators; at other times it steals unashamedly from rival animals' larders; and one of its favourite pastimes is filching and swallowing dirty rubbish from dust-bins. But in wild Nature such behaviour is perfectly respectable, Providence having decided ages ago that it takes all sorts to make a world.

And if the Silver-backed Jackal is a thief, it is a gentleman-thief. It commits its robberies openly, sometimes not without courage in the face of much stronger beasts, and with a professional cleverness that is admirable. Moreover, it is a good-looking animal. Its well-cut face, trim sleek body, bushy long tail, and silver-grey 'saddle' topping its rufous coat are handsome features; and its movements as it trots briskly through the bush have eminent grace. A small pack of hunting jackals is a pleasing sportive sight.

Usually two, three or four of them stalk their meals in partnership. Although their principal means of subsistence are rejected scraps of the victims of lions, leopards and other carnivores, jackals often hunt small mammals, reptiles, game birds and other modest prey for themselves. They attack the fawns of large antelopes if they can snatch them unguarded; and sometimes they pursue and capture adult dik-diks. That requires remarkable cunning and skill, for those pigmies are elusive creatures. Other foods which jackals fancy when they get an opportunity are the eggs and chicks of ostriches.

Silver-backed Jackals usually sleep by day, and go foraging at nights; but often they appear in bright sunlight, especially when the whiff or sight of a nearby lion's kill tempts them. Otherwise the nimble animal's sharp, excited hunting cries are heard mostly from dusk until dawn. When I lived in Delhi the yells of the northern Indian species of jackal frequently broke the midnight silence as a pack trotted across the lawn just outside my bedroom window.

A Silver-backed Jackal bitch gives birth to her three or four cubs in a hole in the ground or in a cranny among rocks. Both parents forage devotedly for the family, and when their offspring are very young they feed them by regurgitation. Later they teach the rising generation to hunt, and scavenge, for themselves.

Leopard

Panthera pardus

I have related in my introductory notes the episode at Amboseli when we set forth at crack of dawn in search of a Leopard, and how in the late afternoon, with the aid of a noisy troop of monkeys, we at last caught sight of the beautiful spotted cat, and snapped the portrait shown on the opposite page. As I mentioned there, leopards are as shy and retiring as they are wild, usually disappearing quickly into cover if they think they are being observed by human beings. Moreover, they are normally nocturnal hunters who in any case often withdraw into hiding during daylight. For those reasons they are more difficult to photograph than almost any other large creature in Kenya.

They are also very shrewd. Just as experienced men can 'smell a rat' in some clandestinely threatening situation, so also a leopard can 'smell a man' in suspicious circumstances. For several days at Maralal Rodney Elliott and his expert game-scouts laid out tempting zebra meat for two separate individual leopards known to be living on different hilltops, in an attempt to induce one or the other to make an appearance within range of Chris's camera. He and she sat for hours day after day in well-disguised hides opposite those baits, which were sometimes tied on the ground and at other times hung in a tree. But although in each case the leopard's near presence was evident from vultures gathered in the surrounding tree-tops—obviously aware of it lurking in the undergrowth, and therefore shy about descending to rob it of its prospective booty—it hardly ever showed itself. Once or twice when it ventured to do so in daylight it kept itself half hidden behind logs strewn between it and the patient, ever hopeful, and always frustrated human watchers. But each night at dusk it began to feast on parts of the zebra. It was almost certainly uneasily suspicious of some undesirable presence throughout the day-time.

Leopards usually hunt alone or in couples. Sometimes a beast obtains its food by stealth, stalking with furtive cunning extremely close to its victim, and then making a sudden swift pounce. At other times it achieves its purpose by setting an ambush, crouching up a tree and leaping on its prey from above. Both those techniques differ from the method used by an animal often mistaken for it, the Cheetah, which makes its catches by a sustained long sprint across open ground.

In addition to being wary, the leopard is an audacious beast. Among its favourite foods are villagers' calves, goats and sheep; and it will take great risks to bag them from farm-yard enclosures. It is also fond of dog-flesh, and many an astonished owner has seen a leopard suddenly leap over a verandah rail, or even through a bungalow window, to snatch his pet from under his eyes. These robberies sometimes cause unpleasant encounters between the big cat and Man which give it a not undeserved reputation for dangerous ferocity. The number of such incidents is increased by the fact that the leopard's

taste for domestic animals often persuades it to live much closer to centres of human habitation, like Nairobi itself, than do lions or other large predators.

The leopard's accomplishment as a tree climber makes it a dangerous enemy of its favourite prey, the baboon. It also enjoys eating monkeys. They know that unhappy fact, and never hesitate to express in loud, scolding abuse their disapproval whenever the spotted cat strolls into their view. Leopards exploit their ability to run up tree-trunks for another purpose. To preserve their kills from theft by rival hunters and scavengers they often carry those corpses into trees, using the high branches as larders.

Death is naturally as common as life in Kenya's wild game sanctuaries. The chief glory of those lovely places is their untamed landscapes filled with free-roaming animals in multitudes unmatched anywhere else on Earth. A visitor's prevailing vivid impression is of the boundless quantity and variety of life in this world. Yet all the time death stalks there. Every now and then one comes across it in the form of the massively horned detached skull of a buffalo, the bleached, broken skeleton of an antelope, the severed wings of a beautiful bird, or some other mangled corpse lying in the grass. Occasionally one sees the actual slaughter being committed—a pack of wild dogs giving chase to a gazelle, a hawk pouncing on a helpless rodent, a pair of cheetahs enjoying a hearty meal at their kill, a mob of vultures observing hopefully the death agonies of some stricken monster—and all sorts of other such sights. They are reminders that in wild Nature life is in fact perpetually dependent on death.

Sooner or later all the most cunning and powerful killers meet the same fate as they deal out to their victims—and frequently by similar violence. Suddenly, unexpectedly one comes upon a glimpse of that truth. Thus it was with the leopard lying asleep on the opposite page. Its eyes were closed in eternal sleep. We discovered it on open ground at Maralal. The body was so fresh that it could not have died more than a few hours earlier. Expert examination of the corpse established that the leopard had probably suffered for two or three days from an ailment which prevented it from eating, for its stomach was completely empty. Then in a weakened, desperate condition it must have got involved in a duel with some horned animal like an eland, and received a wound in its throat which suffocated it. So it lay down and died.

Lion

Panthera leo

In writing about lions one has to start somewhere in their enthralling story, and perhaps the best place to start is at the very beginning of a lion cub's life, which is at its conception during its parents' honeymoon. The pictures on the opposite page illustrate that blissful occasion. Any trippers to Nairobi's National Park can witness it from their car, if their arrival happens to coincide with the nuptials.

Sometimes the bride and bridegroom perform their mating amidst the members of their pride, with the others looking on; but usually they withdraw to enjoy a few consecutive days of love-making in privacy together. During that period they neither hunt nor feed, being entirely absorbed in each other's company, and in their diverting occupation. The pair shown here were typical of all such amorous couples. The lioness spent most of her time stretched at full length snoozing in the grass, whilst the lion sat a few feet away solicitously guarding her, usually with his head watchfully erect, but occasionally also closing his eyes and dozing. About every half-hour throughout the greater part of each day he would rise, stroll purposefully to her, and waken her by a sniff or nuzzle at her posterior. Sometimes she at first gave a snarl of objection at that disturbance, or even made an irritated snap at him; but usually her mood was compliant. After the preliminary contact the lion would lift his face heavenwards, and give an ecstatic sort of yawn. Then the lioness rose to her four feet, walked a few paces, and crouched on the ground. He mounted her, and their mating was completed in less than twenty seconds. Afterwards the lion sauntered back to his sentry post, whilst the lioness rolled over contentedly on her side, and resumed her snoozing. A series of some of these incidents is shown on the opposite page.

After several days a honeymoon couple grow hungry, start hunting again, and return to their pride. Three and a half months later the lioness gives birth to a litter of cubs. In the meantime the lion has probably mated in similar style with another female in the pride, unless he has wandered away in pursuit of some lady-love elsewhere. The family relationship between males and females differs from time to time and from place to place, no doubt according to local circumstances. Often a lion, or two or three lions, remains with the same group of lionesses and their cubs for many months, or longer; whilst at other times their liaison is more fleeting. In the introductory notes to this book I have already given a glimpse of family life in a pride consisting of one lion, three lionesses, and five cubs.

What is almost always long-lived is the bond between a group of lionesses and their cubs; although even that is not invariable. In recent times there was a lioness in Nairobi National Park who would have an affair with a lion, produce the resultant litter, promptly leave her youngsters in the care of another lioness who obligingly assumed responsibility for their upbringing, and go off to another affair with some other lion. The African game-scouts in the park nicknamed her 'The harlot'.

Normally, however, a mother lioness and one or more 'auntie' lionesses combine to care in partnership together for their respective growing cubs until the youngsters can fend for themselves, and depart to live their own lives. The juveniles do that at the age of about twenty months. Meanwhile each mother may well have become pregnant once more following further honeymoons. Infant lions usually depend on their mother's, or occasionally some aunt's, milk for nourishment throughout anything between seven and ten months after birth; but during that time they have licked and chewed at many a kill, and steadily acquired a taste for the meat on which they will rely for the rest of their lives. In the meantime, too, they have watched their adult female relatives hunting, and so begun to study the art. When they are weaned their elders begin to train them seriously in it. Those lessons are interesting to watch, and sometimes amusing; for at first the youngsters make clumsy mistakes, trying to stalk their prey from the wrong direction in relation to the wind, or failing to remain statuesquely motionless when the intended victim first suspects their approach and glances up at them, or starting their final rush-assault too early. Gradually, however, by a process of trial and error under their tutors' expert guidance they improve their techniques.

Not all adult lions associate in prides. Quite often a lion or lioness remains solitary, when it hunts by itself. Sometimes, too, a small group of young males, not yet mating, keep company together; and they depend on their own combined energy and skill to catch their food. But usually the beasts consort in prides of anything from half-a-dozen to about thirty animals, consisting of lions, lionesses and youngsters of various ages, all closely collaborating together. The latter-sized party is rare in most regions, a normal number being more like a dozen beasts. And in all those companies the lionesses, not the lions, are by custom the chief hunters.

Nothing in Nature is more enthralling to watch than the clever, co-ordinated strategy of a pride on the hunt. Hunting lions adopt the method of cats, not of dogs; they stalk cunningly instead of chasing blatantly. Their sight is extremely good, and often they spy and select their prey from a considerable distance. Then the party divides, each adult individual going to perform its particular function. The males act as the beaters, and the females as the killers in the operation. Furtively the separate lionesses proceed to various respective positions down-wind from their chosen victims, where no whiff of themselves will betray their presence to the herd of zebras, wildebeests or other grazing animals. Creeping cautiously behind concealing dips in the ground, among convenient patches of bushes, or through stretches of long grass, they gradually approach their target. If one of the grazers glances up in their direction, they instantly freeze into absolute immobility. When it is reassured, and resumes its feeding, they move forward again with extreme caution; and eventually they reach selected concealments where collectively they form an ambush. After that the male lions do their part of the job, executing the easier tactic of getting into position up-wind from the herd, whence their scent is borne to it. That causes it sudden concern, followed by alarm, which makes the frightened animals scamper away in the direction of the hiding lionesses. Those murderesses choose one or more of the stampeders

as they come near, and suddenly leap from short range to the attack. Usually they deal out death quickly, although their male comrades sometimes arrive in time to perform the final *coup de grâce*.

The ruse does not always work. Sometimes for one reason or another the intended victims escape; but they get slaughtered often enough to meet all the lions' requirements. And when a quarry is dead, and the feast lies spread, the lionesses who have done the most difficult and skilful part of the work withdraw to make room for their lords. With masculine arrogance the males usually insist on eating their share of the banquet before the females and youngsters can claim any part of it; and so the 'women and children' wait a little distance away until those masters have gorged themselves almost to bursting point. Then the lions retire a few paces, lie down, and start to snooze; and the lionesses and cubs go to take their turn at the carcass.

At such a meal they will all eat until their bellies look uncomfortably swollen. Usually that satisfies them for a few days, and they do not hunt again during the interval. But if a pride is large, and one kill does not yield enough meat to indulge all its members to such saturation point, a further hunt takes place sooner. Lions slay only for eating, and not for the sport of killing. Indeed, their dispositions seem to be lazy, and in between hunts most adults lie around in complete idleness, seeming utterly unemployed and bored.

Lions are endowed with keen senses of hearing and smell as well as of sight; so they are efficient hunters by night as well as by day. One magnificent picture on the previous page shows a lioness starting a stalk at dusk. The second shows another lioness suckling her cubs in the evening light. And in the lower photograph opposite a third huntress at her kill has just slapped off an impertinent vulture which tried to snatch a bite of her meat. The thwarted bird has leapt into the air, whilst other, less daring vultures and a jackal hover with patient hopefulness around.

Lions are definitely more powerful than any other predators throughout Africa's length and breadth. Leopards and cheetahs have specialist attributes which make them abler in certain particular techniques, such as climbing trees or sustained sprinting; but in general lions are more masterful. Should any suggestion of rivalry develop, all other hunters will run away from them.

In different regions lions' favourite foods will vary, largely according to the local supply. On East Africa's plains wildebeests and zebras are plentiful, and are most often selected; but in some other areas impalas or buffaloes are more populous and popular. And there are few animals which at one time or another do not fall victim to lions' voracious appetites, from locusts, quails, fish, pythons, baboons and wild pigs to crocodiles, ostriches, giraffes, hippopotamuses, rhinoceroses and elephants. But usually only the young or weak among the latter few species are attacked, and as a consequence older members of those breeds sometimes initiate hostile action against lions lurking in their neighbourhoods. The supposed king of beasts treats such unfriendliness by rhinoceroses and elephants in particular with healthy respect, slinking away from threatening monsters whose ultimate physical superiority he apparently concedes.

Monitor Lizard

Varanus exanthematicus

Two species of Monitor Lizards occur in Kenya; the Nile Monitor which haunts lake and river edges, and the Savannah Monitor which inhabits more arid regions. The former is the wholesale devourer of crocodiles' eggs which I have mentioned in an earlier essay—although it is even fonder of guzzling dead fish washed up along watery shores. It is an enormous lizard, growing in full maturity to a length of five feet or more.

The Savannah Monitor Lizard—which appears on the opposite page—is a rather smaller creature. Nevertheless, it too looks a monstrosity as it waddles across a road and breaks into a wriggling, panicky run if it is startled. The reports of many visitors to places like Tsavo Park that they have seen a crocodile taking the air on dry land several miles away from water usually spring from sudden views of this other reptile. The animal's primeval appearance makes it look like a relic of the pre-historic world, a lingering, out-of-date, one-time contemporary of the dinosaurs who lived more than 70 million years ago, and who survive now only in the form of fossils buried in ancient strata beneath the earth's present surface.

The Savannah Monitor's taste is more varied than that of its Nile cousin, for it keeps itself alive on plentiful supplies of insects, mice, rats, birds' eggs, birds, frogs and other small animals. I can glean no intelligence from books or conversations about its breeding habits. Often I have seen these lizards creeping in and out of subterranean tunnels burrowed into large ant-hills like the one shown on the opposite page; and it may be that their youngsters are born in such secret places. No one seems to have seen a mother Savannah Monitor with her child; but we can feel sure that, in spite of each individual lizard's appearance of being about a million years old, the survival of the species is in fact due to its more frequent periodical reproduction down the ages.

Vervet Monkey

Cercopithecus aethiops

This mischievous character is common in all Kenya's National Parks and Game Reserves. A gregarious creature which usually consorts in lively parties of between twenty and thirty members, it is not addicted to dense forest, but inhabits thinner copses, wooded areas along river banks, and other similar regions. Catholic in its taste for food, it lives on grubs, insects, spiders, fruits of all kinds, leaves and seeds of various trees, the eggs and chicks of nesting birds, certain sorts of gum, and other indiscriminate fare. Nor does it spurn the menus of human picnickers if it gets the slightest chance to adopt such a change of diet. It is an expert and (of course) conscienceless thief who grabs sandwiches, biscuits, cakes, sausages and anything else in sight, if their owners are so careless as to turn their backs for a fraction of a second on an open picnic-basket.

Most parties of the monkeys include several mothers with babies. The wrinkly-faced little ones cling to their parents' backs or bellies as they scamper through the undergrowth. Those juveniles seem to have an unappeasable hunger, for much of the time they just squat imbibing their mothers' milk. A female's two teats are close together, and usually her youngster grips the pair of them in its mouth at once, sucking from both at the same time.

These monkeys' principal enemies are certain eagles in the sky, and all leopards on the ground. At the sight of a leopard they will leap into tree-tops and chatter and scold in vehement protest. Keeping their frightened eyes on the foe, they will prance along the branches, and jump from tree to tree as they follow its progress whilst it strolls with apparent contemptuous indifference along the ground below. Such jibber-jabbering uproars are unfailing clues to a leopard's presence in a vicinity, and they help a human searcher to track and catch sight of the beautiful spotted cat.

But the monkeys' resort to high trees in such situations is not necessarily a withdrawal to security, for leopards also are accomplished climbers, being almost as much at home up tree-trunks as vervets are themselves. And sometimes the hunter on the open ground is acting in cooperation with a colleague in the woodland. It will deliberately lead the monkeys onwards to a place where that partner leopard lies in ambush, ready to make a swift pounce on an unsuspecting victim lured within reach.

Vervet Monkeys do not inhabit only Kenya's wilder places. They are resident also in populous, settled areas like Nairobi's suburbs. Indeed, they penetrate into the capital itself, for I have often exchanged mutually surprised stares with these monkeys in a copse in the grounds of Government House.

Speckled Mousebird
Colius striatus

Small flocks of Speckled Mousebirds are common in Kenya's gardens, where they are unpopular with the owners because the birds' tastes make them very destructive of flowers, fruits and vegetables alike. And they consume more than horticultural products. My suspicion of that was aroused one morning when I noticed a mousebird perched on a bough not far from a Bronzy Sunbird's nest which I was keeping under observation. I believed the hen sunbird was about to lay an egg, and I felt uneasy at the mousebird's seemingly sinister interest.

On the following day my apprehension was confirmed. Arriving near the nest, I was surprised to see the female sunbird clinging motionless to its entrance, neither proceeding to hop indoors nor turning to fly away, as she would have done if she had been engaged on her ordinary business. Instead she gazed intently at some object near by; and following her gaze I saw that she was eyeing a Speckled Mousebird standing two feet away. Although the mousebird appeared indifferent, I felt that it was very conscious of the sunbird's hostile stare. Neither bird moved for two whole minutes; then suddenly the little sunbird loosed her grip on the nest, and flew with fury at her much larger neighbour. That intruder shifted a few inches sideways to evade the assault—and afterwards the two resumed their unfriendly but motionless confrontation of each other. Then a third character suddenly appeared on the scene. Descending like a bolt from the blue, the sunbird's mate launched a dive-bombing attack on the mousebird—which promptly took wing and fled. The cock sunbird chased it for a while, and afterwards returned to his partner. They flew together to a branch above their nest, where they perched companionably side by side. He gazed in lordly fashion around the prospect, whilst she began to preen her feathers.

I knew then that the mousebird must be an egg thief or a chick killer; for in my experience birds always recognise their foes, tolerating species that do them no harm, and showing hostility only to real enemies.

A few days later the sunbirds deserted their nest, and when I sought the reason I found a large hole punched through its wall.

Afterwards I read in Macworth Praed's and Grant's book* that Speckled Mousebirds 'are not always the nice friendly birds they seem; Colonel Pitman had long suspected them, owing to the fact that they are much mobbed by small birds, and he has now actually seen one rip open a Sunbird's nest and carry off the young to devour'.

Perhaps my mousebird had its own youngsters to feed—hungry little nestlings like the twins in the cosy family party shown on the opposite page.

* *Birds of Eastern and North Eastern Africa*, by Macworth Praed and Grant.

190

Gaboon Nightjar

Caprimulgus fossii

One day at Maralal we found the two-chicked nest shown here. The mother nightjar was sitting on it. Confident in her camouflage, she continued to squat tight until one of us stepped within two feet of her. Then she rose and fluttered away on silent wings. We snipped the immediately surrounding long grasses, so as to clear a view for photography.

Chris and Rodney were busy with a leopard; so she could not attend to the nightjars until towards dusk. An adult bird was then sitting on the nest, and remained so whilst we erected a camera on a tripod barely nine feet away. But when we advanced to establish flashlamps four feet nearer, it leapt into the air. We quickly erected a hide; Chris installed herself inside it; and the rest of us withdrew to concealment behind bushes. A minute later we saw first one parent nightjar and then both flying above the nest. They continued for some time to glide in small circles round the spot. Dusk grew deeper, and to us the birds became mere silhouettes as at each lap they dipped lower towards the ground. I expected that one would pluck up courage to alight there . . . . Then suddenly Chris called to me to go and put the chicks back on the nest!

As I approached she whispered that whenever an adult bird flew close she heard it call softly to the chicks—and soon afterwards she had detected a commotion, and realised that they were leaving home. Searching, I found them hiding in long grass two feet behind the nest. I picked them up, and replaced them in their cradle. Chris took pictures of them such as the one opposite; but it was evidently now vain to expect an adult to return; so we demolished the hide and departed, hoping that the nightjars would recover confidence in time for photography without flashlamps the next morning.

Sure enough, a parent was then sitting again on the original site. But when Chris appeared cautiously a dozen feet away, it flew off. She too left at once, to let it regain assurance. On returning later, however, she found the nest deserted. She walked up to it—and suddenly a nightjar leapt from the grass just beyond it. She saw the chicks squatting on the exact spot where I had recovered them the previous evening.

Chris and Rodney left on another leopard hunt whilst I put the chicks back on their nest, and withdrew to watch developments from hiding. I hoped to see a parent return and coddle them; but instead I heard one start calling its monotonous 'tok, tok, tok . . .' from distant trees. It kept repeating the refrain. For some time the chicks lay dozing; but after a while they opened their eyes, and shuffled back into concealment two feet away. No doubt they were obeying a call to retreat.

That afternoon a nightjar was once more sitting with its youngsters on the original nest; but at the slightest provocation they repeated their short withdrawal into cover. We got no more photographs.

Fringe-eared Oryx

Oryx beisa callotis

Usually Fringe-eared Oryxes are shy, wary creatures who take to rapid flight whenever a strange visitor halts to watch them; but for some reason the animals pictured here were less suspicious. Perhaps they had become accustomed to the approach of incorrigible human beings with field-glasses and cameras in Amboseli Reserve, where they were members of a wild resident herd. Whatever the reason, they and the rest of their party did not show undue alarm and disappear at a swift gallop at our appearance. Instead they stood stock still whilst our vehicle bumped slowly over rough ground towards them, eyeing us with as much curiosity as nervousness, and only turning tail and cantering unhastily away when we came quite near them. When we stopped they, too, soon stopped; and when we started to move cautiously forward once more, they again stayed eyeing us until they decided that we were drawing uncomfortably close, when with evident reluctance they turned their backs on us and ambled onwards yet again. Gradually they became used to our presence, and gained confidence about our harmless intentions. Then they began to loiter for longer intervals during our careful pursuit of them, and to pose in graceful natural groups in the open, scrub-dotted landscape beneath a wide sky.

These normally shy, large antelopes associate in herds of anything between half-a-dozen and three dozen beasts, often consisting mostly of cows and calves. Sometimes bulls lead a solitary existence. Fringe-eared Oryxes are fairly common in many areas in Kenya south of the Tana River. Their cousins the Beisa Oryxes inhabit more northerly regions in the country; and these are similar in character and habits. The bulls of both breeds are strong as well as hefty brutes; and the skin covering their shoulders is so tough that it is coveted by certain African warrior tribes as excellent material for making trusty shields.

The oryxes themselves are no mean fighters. Their long, sharp, rapier-like horns are formidable weapons, which grow rather larger on cows than on bulls, and which they use to good effect against all sorts of enemies. Many a lion has been mortally wounded by one of their vicious jabs.

Ostrich

Struthio camelus

The ostrich is peculiar to Africa. It used to exist also in Arabia; but now it is extinct there. Two different sub-species inhabit Kenya, the Masai Ostrich with naked pink neck and thighs, and the Somali Ostrich whose skin pigment is blue-grey. One or two other minor differences also exist between them. A full-grown bird of either type stands between seven and eight feet high. It is flightless; but what it lacks in speed with its beautifully ornate wings it makes up for on its long, swift-pacing legs. An ostrich in a hurry has been timed to run considerable distances at forty-five miles per hour.

The male is polygamous, and all the hens mating with one cock lay their eggs in the same nest on bare ground. Each hen is said to lay between fourteen and sixteen eggs, and as many as ninety-four have been recorded on one nest in the Libyan desert. Usually a clutch is considerably smaller. Nevertheless the number is often so great that a sitting bird cannot incubate them all. The superfluous ones are pushed out of the nest, and lie neglected on the surrounding earth.

A cock and his spouses each take turns at incubation. When I approached a nest in the Nairobi National Park a hen on the job gave an impressive demonstration of the correct interpretation of the phrase about an ostrich hiding its head in the sand. From fifteen yards away I would not have known that the largest bird in the world—or the smallest bird either, for that matter—was sitting there. All I saw was what appeared to be a chunk of rock protruding from the foot-high grass. Slowly I realised that this was in fact the back of a mother ostrich whose long neck and head were stretched flat along the ground in front of her, invisible to me. With considerable justification she hoped that I could not see, or at least recognise, her.

After watching her stay thus motionless for a considerable time I drove in my land-rover to within four feet of her. As I approached very close she abandoned her pretence at non-existence, raised her head upright, and gazed at me inquisitively through her large, brightly shining eyes. Otherwise she did not budge an inch or twitch a feather. Thus we scrutinised each other, both unmoving, for five long minutes. Only when my vehicle's engine started up again did the bird rise, trot a dozen paces away, flop down on the ground, and once more 'hide her head in the sand'.

I stooped, and counted twenty-three warm eggs which had lain beneath her body. Another twenty-one dead cold ones were scattered just beyond the nest's rim.

As soon as the coddled eggs hatch, the bevy of tiny chicks start wandering through the surrounding country under the joint guidance of the cock and a hen. They remain together as a family party for many months—as grotesquely charming a sight as any on Earth.

The portrait opposite is of a male Masai Ostrich sauntering in the Nairobi National Park.

Verreaux's Eagle Owl

Bubo lacteus

I have caught sight of this handsome eagle owl, more than two feet tall, asleep at mid-day in a densely foliaged acacia tree; and occasionally at nights I have heard its loud 'hu-hu-hu-hu . . .' break the silence in an ascending scale of mournful notes. It sometimes also draws attention to itself by emitting a high-pitched screech combined with a sharp clicking noise. But to appreciate fully its splendid horned head, large lustrous eyes, imperiously hooked beak, and beautifully vermiculated plumage one has, alas, to see it in captivity. The bird shown here is being held by its owner, David Roberts, in his menagerie on the shores of Lake Baringo. I often admired it there as it gazed back at me with a look as solemn as that of a sagacious philosopher, yet through eyes as glamorous as those of a gorgeous young movie-star.

One afternoon the door of its cage was left accidentally unlatched, and the bird escaped into a near-by tree. There it was forced to stay by a crowd of much smaller birds, which immediately mobbed it. Whenever it stretched its wings to fly away their fussy hubbub became particularly threatening, some Black Drongos being especially offensive in the insults which they hurled at it. It must have decided that discretion would be the better part of valour until night subdued them and enlivened it, for it promptly closed its wings again, and stayed motionless. But later in the afternoon one of Roberts' African assistants climbed the tree, and reclaimed the absconder. Docilely it surrendered itself into his arms—and now it lives in Frankfurt Zoo in Germany.

Verreaux's Eagle Owl is the largest of African owls. In Kenya's wilds it can be found as high as 8,500 feet up the slopes of Mount Kenya. But it is usually a bird of lower levels, frequenting woodland, bush and savannah country, where every night it hunts a great variety of game such as rodents, snakes, lizards, beetles, poultry, game-birds up to the size of guinea-fowls, and other prey, including prickly hedgehogs. It nests in hollow old tree-trunks, or on a platform of sticks in a tree-fork, or occasionally in the abandoned nest of some other large bird. Usually the hen lays two eggs, which in due course produce minute smoky-grey twins.

Probably owing to its eerie cries in the darkness, this eagle owl is feared by the African natives in many districts; and it plays a sinister part in their legends and superstitions.

White and Pink-backed Pelicans

Pelecanus onocrotalus   Pelecanus rufescens

Two species of large, dignified and fabulous pelicans frequent East Africa—the hefty White Pelican and the smaller Pink-backed Pelican. Both are residents in considerable numbers, whilst the former is also a plentiful winter migrant from Europe and Asia. There is no mistaking the monstrous creatures, with their big, billowing bodies poised on short legs, thick curving necks upholding solemn faces, and long, large beaks with baggy pouches suspended below them. On calm waters the birds float in groups like flotillas of grand old-fashioned frigates in full sail; and in the sky they cruise around with equal ease in ponderous yet graceful air squadrons.

They enjoy flying, their technique being to progress by a series of leisurely wing-beats between short periods of gliding. Sometimes quite large flocks circle on motionless pinions high in the blue, soaring in thermal currents apparently for sheer pleasure. They look less at home on land, where they have a cumbersome appearance accentuated by a somewhat laboured movement when they walk. But on water they are in their true element. Although they are sometimes found in placid bays or lagoons along the coasts, they are not fond of ruffled seas; and so their favourite haunts are mirror-smooth inland lakes. On these they often congregate in considerable numbers.

They are in their element on water because they are born fishermen. Mainly they feed on fish, although they are not averse to gobbling into their ample pouches other fare like frogs. Occasionally they pursue their watery meals singly or in pairs; but more customarily they give chase to the prey in co-operative teams of about a dozen birds. They appear then like a small fishing fleet engaged in trawling. Either as a compact group, or else spread out in a line or half circle to extend the field of their operations, they propel themselves smoothly and steadily across the surface of a lake, driving a school of fish before them towards the shallows. Every now and then they all momentarily check their progress, raise their wings slightly as they tilt their bodies forwards, and plunge their beaks in unison into the depths, either to make a feast of catches or else to frighten the fish onwards. Immediately afterwards they raise their heads again and continue their advance, until by some apparently automatic collective judgement they all resolve that the instant has arrived for another mass ducking. Instantly they halt and submerge their faces once more. So they continue round and round a lake, chasing the fish before them, and gulping them at will. Several of these flotillas may be searching the same comparatively small area of water at the same time, when they appear rather like the Spanish Armada mobilising for its assault on Elizabethan England.

Occasionally the bird adopts a different method of fishing, fluttering momentarily in the air a few feet above the lake's surface, and then diving with a big splash into the water to make a catch.

The picture on the previous page shows a White Pelican in all its pompous dignity, reminiscent of the verse:

> A wonderful bird is the Pelican.
> His bill will hold more than his belly can.
> He can take in his beak
> Food enough for a week.
> But I'm damned if I see how the hell he can.

The top photograph facing this page shows a White Pelican in full flight; and the lower one a mixed flock of several White and one or two Pink-backed Pelicans resting in shallow water in the course of one of their local migrations.

Members of both species usually nest aloft in trees, although occasionally they resort to bushes, and sometimes, in the absence of adequate vegetation in a landscape, they even condescend to lay their eggs on the ground. Their breeding colonies can exist many miles from water, when the parent birds make long daily journeys to fetch their meals. The nests are built of sticks and other convenient materials; and since pelicans seem to be less hygienic than most birds, these nurseries often stink to high heaven. Upon them the mother White Pelicans each deposit a solitary chalky-white egg, whilst Pink-backed Pelicans lay between two and four similar objects of pale blue or white. The chicks which in due course emerge from them are lively young freaks with rather a reptilian appearance. Only in those domestic family parties do pelicans find their voices. At other seasons they are silent birds; but at their nests White Pelicans utter occasional grunting notes, whilst the Pink-backed variety emits a series of guttural croaks.

At the right seasons many family groups of these imposing creatures can be seen on and round the lakes along the Great Rift Valley. And almost always on Lake Nakuru small flotillas of pelicans mix freely with multitudinous fleets of flamingos—a most splendid nautical sight.

Blacksmith Plover

Hoplopterus armatus

This decorative creature lives in considerable numbers beside freshwater streams, swamps and lakes. It is said to be shy; and certainly if one approaches a flock in normal circumstances they rise quickly and fly away, uttering loud alarm calls. But the bird's instinct to retreat is remarkably restrained when it is sitting on eggs. We came upon a Blacksmith Plover squatting suspiciously like an incubating mother on open ground at Amboseli; and although our land-rover drove to within four feet of it, the gallant creature continued to sit. It eyed us no doubt with apprehension as we loomed above it; but it never so much as flickered a feather. Even when Chris made the necessary movement to focus her camera, and when the camera clicked half-a-dozen times as she took pictures, the bird did not stir. Only a while later did it rise deliberately and stroll away—leaving behind it three spotted eggs in a shallow scrape in the ground lined with grasses.

I think this was a routine departure at a moment when the plover's mate should have come to take a turn at incubation, for that partner had appeared, and was circling round the nest ten yards away. But it would not come nearer, evidently being more nervous than its colleague. Probably it was the cock, for among many species of birds in similar circumstances the male is more timid than the female.

Now the hen (if the first bird was the hen) behaved in a remarkable manner. As she walked slowly away she picked up bits of earth, animal manure, and grass in her beak, and threw them backwards towards the nest. She continued to do so even when she had gone some distance away, and they fell far short of it. At the same time she started uttering subdued, slightly alarmed clucks. Was this some delayed reflex action of fright at the presence of the monstrous land-rover beside her eggs? And was she instinctively, or symbolically, trying to conceal them beneath little bits of earth, dung and grass? Her nervous reaction seemed infectious, for her mate hovering uncertainly in the background also began to peck frequently at the soil. And three times he flew with irate aggression at a few sandpipers standing beside a pool some distance away, where they could not possibly constitute any threat to the nest.

That second bird never plucked up courage to come and do incubation duty. Instead the first plover kept returning to the nest, sitting on the eggs for a few moments, and then rising and departing once more. Possibly it was confused by a conflict of instincts: partly a wish to induce the other plover by example to come and sit with impunity, and partly an inclination to resume protection of the eggs itself.

Crowned Plover or Lapwing

Stephanibyx coronatus

Like the Blacksmith Plover of which I have just written, this Crowned Plover laid her eggs on bare earth in the middle of the Amboseli plain; and like that other plover, also, she refused to budge from her nest when we drove right up to it in our land-rover. Indeed, she would not rise and depart even when later we clapped our hands, shouted at her, and made other persuasive attempts through the car window to shoo her away. Chris had by then taken all the pictures she wanted of the bird sitting on the nest, and she wished to get some studies of it approaching its eggs on its long, elegant legs. But the plover flatly refused to collaborate, continuing to squat stodgily on the ground.

Then it and I together devised a method by which we co-operated in a plan to get Chris the pictures she wanted. When she was ready to take a snapshot I stepped from the land-rover and took a step towards the plover. It could not tolerate this intrusion by a strange two-legged animal, as distinct from the four-wheeled creatures to which it had become accustomed in Amboseli Reserve; and it promptly rose and ran away. I then climbed back into the vehicle, and it as abruptly turned and strolled back towards the little scrape in the earth containing three eggs which was its nest. The two of us repeated that performance with regularly reiterated precision in every detail several times—until Chris had got all the photographs she desired.

The bird's action on each occasion when it arrived back at the nest was engaging. Its last two or three steps were always slow and cautious. Then it would stand above the nest, look down at the eggs to make sure that they were still in position, straddle its feet wider apart on either side of them, and very, very gradually lower its body, until it finally settled plumb on the eggs. Incidentally, they were half-buried in earth, and their camouflage colouring was so effective that during the plover's absences, even when we knew exactly where to look for them, we found difficulty in recognising them.

Crowned Plovers are well-known for their bravery. They often utter scolding yells of protest at anyone who presumes to walk across their territory, and they make vicious dive-bombing attacks at dogs trespassing near their nests. Probably that is because their eggs are sometimes raided and eaten by various types of predators, and the birds think they have recognised a new potential enemy.

Plovers will sometimes heap abuse on larger and more fearsome beasts than dogs. I have watched a party of half-a-dozen Blacksmith Plovers furiously mobbing a cheetah—an action worthy of gaining them the ornithological equivalent of the V.C. for courage.

Long-toed Plover or Lapwing

Hemiparra crassirostris

This is a very shy member of the plover family which has not often posed for its photograph. It is an interesting as well as graceful bird, because it appears to be in process of changing its habits in the long course of the evolution of its species, adapting itself to new types of living quarters. Possibly in past ages it was more of a shore and ground bird, like other plovers and lapwings; and in some regions it is still primarily an earthbound creature of that type. But in many areas it has become a water bird to the extent of strolling across the surfaces of lakes on thin rafts of floating vegetation such as clumps of water-lilies. It has developed large, long-toed feet like a jacana, and is in fact becoming more of a lily-trotter than a landlubber.

The bird is not uncommon at Amboseli, where one or two can usually be found at pools scattered here and there across the plain. It is pleasant to sit beside one of those miniature lakes watching a rhinoceros nibbling breast-deep at reeds in the water, a submerged hippopotamus occasionally surfacing to take a breath of air, wild ducks, grebes and cormorants disporting on the pool, egrets, crakes and herons hunting prey along its shores —and then to catch sight of a Long-toed Plover running across a thin lily floor on the water's surface as it chases grasshoppers, beetles and molluscs among the leaves. At Amboseli—where the photograph opposite was taken—the species has lost a lot of its pristine shyness, and shows more confidence in the friendliness of Man. When alarmed it usually takes swiftly to its heels instead of its wings. If it does fly, it utters a loud metallic 'tik, tik' as it goes.

The bird's nest is a well-constructed platform of weeds and debris marooned in shallow water, and firmly anchored to the swamp-bed by a painstaking build-up of vegetable matter as a foundation. On it a hen lays two or three spotted and streaked eggs.

Bohor Reedbuck
Redunca redunca

This reedbuck's normal habitat is either in swampy country with plentiful reeds or papyrus, or else on open grassland at altitudes of about 8,000 feet or more. A medium-sized antelope, it is usually seen singly or in pairs, although sometimes it consorts in small parties of about half-a-dozen animals. One of its distinguishing features is the pair of horns hooked sharply forwards, which it shares with other species of reedbucks distributed through Africa. In its case the horns are even more abruptly hooked than in those others, and they are worn only by the males. Shy and nervous, when disturbed these spry reedbucks canter quickly away with a strange 'rocking-horse' gait caused by them throwing their legs out widely fore-and-aft as they run. Often they utter a series of whistling cries as they depart.

The Bohor Reedbuck shown on the opposite page had grown a bit—though not much—tamer owing to confinement in a large water-side enclosure among David Roberts's collection of wild beasts and birds assembled at Lake Baringo. With two or three others of its kind it had made itself at home there—but it was still very disinclined for any undue familiarity with human beings. Only in the case of David himself would it make a concession, provided that he met it half-way by bringing a bribe in the form of a favourite foodstuff which did not grow in its natural surroundings. That delicacy was nothing more than a slice of dry bread, for which it had developed a passion! Induced by this temptation, it would come to David like any farmyard calf, and nibble crumbs from his hands. But it never acquired an air of relaxed confidence, and was always ready to shy away nervously at the slightest unaccustomed gesture.

One of its companions in captivity in David's spacious wild domain is a male animal of the same species. I hear that the pair mated not long ago; and so as I write this note the beast shown opposite has become an expectant mother.

Reeve

Philomachus pugnax

This photograph was taken at Amboseli during the last few days of April. An initiated reader will notice that the reeve shown in it is wearing her bridal dress. Yet ruffs and reeves do not breed in Africa. This bird was in fact about to migrate to some region of Europe or Asia where the members of the clan mate, build nests, and produce their young. Similar conduct is true of various other types of waders who are only winter visitors to East Africa, and who go to more northerly climes to propagate their species. They almost all assume their beautiful breeding plumage just before they leave Africa.

That does not apply to the reeve's male partner, the ruff. It is true that his feathers start a slight moult just before he migrates, some areas of his upper parts and belly beginning to change colour from grey and light brown to darker brown and black. But the impressively large, erectile ear-tufts and ruff (which gives him his name) do not develop until after his arrival in Europe or Asia. No doubt that is because those fabulous adornments would interfere with convenient, speedy flight during his several thousand miles journey. They start to grow only after he lands on his breeding ground, when the time has come for them to perform their function in attracting the attention and inducing the compliance of a female. Nature is very considerate in her arrangements of all such details.

The reeve shown here was busily searching for food in a pool. With remarkable zeal she paddled wader-style in the shallows, and occasionally swam like a phalarope in deeper water as she turned this way and that in her hunting. Every few moments she jabbed her beak into the pond and captured a prize. The species feeds on aquatic flies and other water or land insects. Probably this particular bird was storing up layers of fat to give her the necessary energy for her long travels, as migrants customarily do immediately before they set forth. The reeve's nuptial plumage showed that she was ready to depart, her bridal dress being also her going-away costume.

Although all the breeding ruffs and reeves leave Africa when spring is in the air, large numbers of non-breeding members of the species remain in various parts of the continent throughout the year. Their weddings are postponed for another twelve months.

Black Rhinoceros

Diceros bicornis

The once very populous rhinoceros family spread across various countries round the world has been mercilessly persecuted by Man because of the supposed aphrodisiac qualities of its horns. The prolific Chinese people in particular long believed—and, as I know from Chinese friends in south-east Asia, in some cases still believe—in the rejuvenating potency of rhino horn. Enormous sums of money have therefore been given for this imaginary magical virtue; and as a result several species of rhinoceroses in India, Nepal, Burma, Malaya, Java and Sumatra exist precariously, in grave danger of extermination. Those are mostly beasts with short, single horns.

Two other species reside in Africa, both wearing long double horns. They are called the Black and the White Rhinoceros respectively, although neither of them is either black or white, since both sport hides coloured a sort of battleship grey. That is not their only gunboat-like attribute. The Black species in particular can be very aggressive in defence of its family, and has been known to charge and send sprawling such intruders into its territory as 3-ton lorries. Its own weight is about one ton, which gives it a considerable power when advancing against a foe at its attacking speed of nearly twenty-five miles per hour. Its most potent weapons are not its horns, but its hefty shoulders. A shove from one of them is an unforgettable—and sometimes an incurable—experience.

The horn is not made of bone, but of tightly congealed hair. It is therefore not unbreakable, and sometimes it gets smashed in the domestic fights which are a part of rhinoceros courtships. Incidentally, unlike most animals, the rhino seems to be strictly and devotedly monogamous. The horn often grows longer on females than on males, and the record specimen of modern times was said to be the more than four feet, six inches long horn which graced the snout of a famous animal called Gertie at Amboseli—although some pundits aver that her companion Gladys's implement was even longer before it got chipped.

The front horn is sometimes employed as an aid to feeding. I have watched a rhinoceros using it so effectively as a plough to cut furrows through the earth in search of salt that I wondered whether a similar sight could have given primitive man his first idea of inventing the simple wooden plough.

A rhinoceros' eyesight is bad, but its sense of smell is acute; and chiefly through its nostrils it detects the comings and goings of other creatures. It has no serious enemy except Man; but as a result of that hostility the African White Rhinoceros is now on the danger list for extinction. Its smaller Black cousin (shown on the opposite page rising from a mud bath) is commoner; but it also is declining in numbers. Both these interesting, rather pre-historic-looking monstrosities must be religiously protected.

Robin Chat

Cossypha caffra

Except for some male sunbirds, the Robin Chat is perhaps the most beautiful small bird in my Nairobi garden; and it is certainly the sweetest songster there. Its melodious phrases are warbled with the serene clarity of recitatives by a prima donna; and they often cheer me as I sit imprisoned by official duty in my study.

I have kept a watch on three separate Robin Chats' nests in the garden; but each of them in turn came to grief. Once the deep-cupped nest was punctured from below, and its eggs stolen by some furtive enemy; and twice the hatched chicks were kidnapped when they were only a few days old. Perhaps the former pirate was a Speckled Mousebird; and probably the latter was a Fiscal Shrike which treats my garden as its private hunting lodge, and indeed its slaughterhouse.

The nest portrayed opposite had also suffered a tragedy, but of a different sort. When its clutch of robin chats' eggs were laid, a hen Red-chested Cuckoo paid a brief, surreptitious visit to it, and contributed one more egg to the collection. After the infant cuckoo hatched it could not tolerate any rivals in its cradle, and heaved the other chicks out of the nest one by one. It is the monstrous creature almost bursting from the grass-cup on the opposite page.

Being such a size, and growing lustier every day, it had a ravenous appetite. Its smaller foster-parents had their work cut out to keep it satisfied. They both brought food to it every few minutes, and their labours continued ceaselessly hour after hour; yet all the time the young giant yelled piteously for more, as if it were perpetually on the verge of starvation. Its digestion, however, was evidently working well, for periodically a robin chat, after inserting an insect into its mouth at one end of its body, extracted a 'faecal sac' from beneath its tail at the other end. Many adult birds perform that service for their chicks, thus keeping their nests hygienically clean. But the prodigious cuckoo's 'sac' was much larger than any robin chat should be asked to carry, bulging hugely from the bird's little beak. I could almost hear the carrier heave a sigh of relief when it dropped the load a few yards away.

Red-chested Cuckoos are residents of Africa. Shy about making any obvious appearance, they usually remain out of sight among foliage; yet they brazenly advertise their presence by shrieking a loud, oft reiterated, three-syllable phrase. As it is uttered mostly in the rainy season, some people believe it to be a prophetic announcement that 'It will rain. It will rain . . .'. So the cuckoo is nick-named the 'Rain bird', although its pronouncements are in fact no more reliable than those of other meteorologists.

Lilac-breasted Roller

Coracias caudata

Like almost all types of rollers in various lands, Africa's Lilac-breasted Roller is a noisy bird with a harsh, sometimes screeching and at other times chuckling voice which it uses enthusiastically whenever it gets excited. Like all other rollers, too, it is a master of trick flying, the male in particular performing astonishing aerial acrobatics when he is courting a desirable female. And again like other rollers, the species usually nests in holes in trees, although it occasionally resorts for that purpose to tunnels in ant-hills.

Another quality which it shares with many members of the family is glorious beauty of plumage. Perhaps its colouring is less theatrical than that of some of its cousins, like the Indian Roller (or Blue Jay) in Asia; but if its brilliance of hue is less dramatic, it is more delicate than the dresses of many of those others. No tinting of feathers could be more subtly gorgeous than the merging of green, blue and lilac on the breast of the bird perched on the opposite page.

When that roller's portrait was taken it was sitting on the topmost branch of a tall, bare, broken tree near the foot of majestic Mount Kilimanjaro. The bird was busily hunting a mid-morning meal; and from its lofty vantage-point it kept a sharp look-out across the ground for fifty yards around. Frequently it spied a lizard, a grasshopper, or some other large insect lurking in the grass. It then quietly spread its wings, fluttered down to earth, captured the delicacy in its beak, and flew back to the tree-top to swallow the protesting creature. It made the down-and-up journey about thirty times in an hour—a typical example of the Lilac-breasted Roller's hearty style of feeding.

The bird sometimes fancies its food cooked rather than raw. If it catches sight of a grass-fire anywhere in a landscape, it will fly whatever great distance is required to feast on the roasted lizards, fried grasshoppers and other scorched meats left by the flames. Its eyesight is extraordinarily sharp, and wherever it sees a coil of smoke it knows that there is fire—and no doubt some tasty chops also.

Chestnut-bellied Sandgrouse

Pterocles exustus

These are birds of the desert and semi-desert. Through the daytime they scatter widely over vast areas; and they can then be flushed singly, in pairs, or in small family parties here, there and everywhere across the arid wilderness. But always in the early mornings— and again each evening during the hottest, driest weather—they gather in multitudinous flocks to enjoy a drinking bout. Often they first assemble at a rendezvous not far from the pool where they customarily slake their thirsts, and then proceed in smaller companies for the refreshment. I have seen assemblies of thousands of birds morning after morning at Wajir, an oasis in the middle of the extensive Northern Frontier District of Kenya to which in the non-rainy season Somali tribesmen bring their caravans of camels for drinks at centuries-old wells. In the compound before the local District Commissioner's house a tiny tank of water sunk in the ground acts as a daily magnet for sandgrouse from many miles around. For an hour or more soon after dawn a continuous succession of flocks of the birds appear like clouds racing across the otherwise speckless blue sky, circle above the splash of water, and then drop down to alight near its edges. By some well-understood system of precedence a few of them at a time advance to take quick, deep drinks, and then make way for the next comers in the queue. Flock after flock go through that procedure as if it were some hallowed ritual.

That daily assembly in tiny, remote Wajir is much more multitudinous than the crowd of pigeons invariably being fed by trippers in London's Trafalgar Square. The analogy is not inappropriate, for although these sandgrouse appear like game-birds, they are in fact closely allied to the pigeon family. And at Wajir's pool they strut on their short legs and carry their plump bodies in rather pompous pigeonish style.

As soon as every member of every group has drunk its fill, the whole flock rises into the air again, and disappears as fast as it arrived. Before long the individuals and pairs have scattered to their separate territories all over the desert. Their daily pub-crawl is over for another twenty-four hours—unless the heat is more thirst-making than usual, when they return for a sun-downer towards the end of each day.

The picture on the opposite page shows how cunning is the protective colouring of these birds, otherwise exposed to easy view across the flat wastes. At a short distance they merge, invisible, into their environment. During the breeding season they do not bother to make even a scrape for a nest, but lay their two or three stone-coloured, speckled eggs on bare, unaltered ground.

Wood Sandpiper
Tringa glareola

Like almost all the other score of varied waders in East Africa, this sandpiper is a winter visitor or passage migrant in those parts. Some non-breeding individuals remain throughout the year, but in the spring all the multitudes of others take wing from their winter resorts near the Equator to distant nesting grounds in the sub-Arctic or the Arctic. So they are much-travelled birds, their trim bodies, strong wings and lively dispositions fitting them well for their twice-yearly globe-trottings.

Wood Sandpipers prefer fresh-water to salt-water feeding grounds; so, unlike many types of waders who crowd along sea-shores, they are uncommon on the coast, dallying instead on the grassy edges of inland swamps and lakes. Again, although many types of waders are highly gregarious and consort in large flocks, this sandpiper is more inclined to keep itself to itself, being usually seen in only ones, twos or threes. It walks and paddles with ceaseless energy, constantly turning its head this way and that in search of food, and frequently bending its head to dip its beak and seize the worms, crustaceans or insects which it likes. If alarmed it utters a pleasant liquid whistle, or a series of sweet trilling notes.

When the time comes for their migration the birds temporarily forget their normal unsociable disposition, and gather in large parties for the journey. Many species of birds on migration hasten mightily, covering hundreds of miles in a few hours; but others are not in any particular hurry, for they must feed themselves periodically on the ground to maintain their strength throughout long and sometimes exhausting travels. Certain extensive, unrewarding regions like the Sahara Desert and the Atlantic Ocean must of course be crossed as swiftly as possible; but elsewhere the travellers incline to take their time. The White Stork, for example, covers only between sixty-five and seventy-five miles a day, taking nearly a hundred days to complete a journey from Europe to South Africa.

The waders, including Wood Sandpipers, usually fly at nights, alighting each morning to feed throughout the day on some well-provisioned lake-shore or river-bank. Certain other species like swallows, martins and swifts travel by day, because they feed on the wing, and so they never need to come down to earth. The sandpipers may take a few weeks to complete their distances of many hundreds of miles. Certain other migrants cross much vaster spaces. Probably the record long-distance traveller is the Arctic Tern, which summers in northern Europe and winters in Antarctica, thus covering more than 20,000 miles on each of its twice-yearly trips.

Secretary Bird

Sagittarius serpentarius

The Secretary Bird acquired its name from a certain primness in dress and demeanour reminiscent of a notorious human type. As it struts across the ground its rather scruffy pate, long feathers protruding from the back of its head like quill-pens stuck over a scribe's ears, and trimly folded grey wings extending neatly into a long grey tail above black thigh feathers make it seem like an old-fashioned private secretary wearing a frock-coat above silk knee-breeches. Its humourless glance and sedate steps complete the likeness.

I have described in my introductory notes the tribulations attending the photography of the lower nest shown opposite. I watched the parent birds hunting food for their nestling. Their 'territory' was vast; later I came across the next-door pair of Secretary Birds inspecting their own estate about a mile away. In both cases the two adults quartered their domain with meticulous care, marching at a steady pace along separate straight lines within twenty yards of each other, and scrutinising every inch of the ground with sharp downcast eyes as they advanced. Suddenly one would halt, lift a foot, and pounce with it, grabbing a victim. Often the bird stamped that foot vigorously several times, knocking the life out of its obstinate captive. Then it would upstretch its wings and flap them to maintain a balance as it stood on one leg and, raising the other foot, lowered its head to transfer the prey from its claws to its mouth. Having swallowed the prize for storage in its gullet until it should regurgitate the morsel later for the nestling, it resumed its forward march in search of another victim.

Chris in her hide beside the nest always received warning of a parent bird's approach, because the young bird would catch sight of its elder from afar, stand up excitedly, gaze keenly in its direction, and occasionally utter an impatient, greedy call. For some reason the adult usually brought in its bill a long twig or other bit of building material, which it dropped on the nest as it alighted. Then the youngster pecked avidly at the old bird's beak, instinctively stimulating it to regurgitate the feast stored within. It promptly spewed an assortment of dead lizards, snakes, mice, frogs and other delicacies on to the nest floor. Both birds set to work to tear them to bits and swallow them, the parent taking its own meal at the same time as its junior. They guzzled in mutual competition; but the older bird naturally demolished the dishes faster than its less expert companion, which sometimes caused the latter to express vigorous annoyance by jabs of its bill.

As soon as the parent had eaten its fill, it spread its wings and flew away, to start hunting for their next meal.

Fiscal Shrike

Lanius collaris

My garden is a happy hunting ground for Fiscal Shrikes, those inveterate slayers of insects, small mammals, reptiles, and other birds' chicks. One pair's territory extends across a lawn and two flower-beds outside my study windows; so I have a ring-side view of their safaris. The cock was the bird that attacked the Laughing Doves' nestling which I have already described on page 98.

The shrikes' nest (portrayed opposite) was lodged in a flowering bougainvillea bush; and so far as I could see the cock did all the nest-building entirely unaided by his mate. He also did most, if not all, the hunting for her food during their courtship and his home-making. I often watched the hen dallying idly on a bough as he slaved for her. He behaved like a most chivalrous, industrious gentleman, whilst she played the part of a lazy slut. But later she made up for that by doing all the incubation of their eggs.

Both then and for some time after their chicks hatched the cock continued to be the family's sole bread-winner. Every few minutes throughout most of each day he arrived at the nest with a fresh supply of food. When the sitting hen saw him approach she fluttered her wings excitedly, and occasionally uttered little exclamations of anticipatory satisfaction. He gave her the meat, and promptly flew away to fetch more. Sometimes she sat and swallowed it herself, and at other times she rose and fed the youngsters squatting beneath her. When they grew older she left the nest now and then to start foraging again for herself; but through most of their domestic home life the cock remained the principal provider.

Since the food was all animal flesh of one kind or another, he engaged in a career of perpetual murder. He established little larders like butchers' shops here and there in the neighbourhood. On the needle-sharp leaves of a sisal plant, for example, I observed corpses of new-born chicks impaled by him; and in a thorny shrub bits and pieces of dead bodies were hung. This habit has earned the Fiscal Shrike the nickname of 'Jacky Hangman', which is the equivalent of the title 'Butcher-bird' for shrikes in Britain.

The male shrike resented the activities of rival murderers, no doubt because he recognised them as threats to his own nestlings. His relations with all Speckled Mousebirds, for instance, were distinctly hostile. Nor did he demonstrate his disapproval only towards birds of his own size. One morning a Kite settled in a tree overlooking his nest; and at once he sallied forth to do battle. Mounting into the air above the Kite, he launched two 'dive-bombing' attacks on it. Each time he passed very close by its head, and I believe he might have struck an actual physical blow if the Kite had not ducked evasively. After the second assault the bird of prey flew into another tree; but the shrike followed it, and launched three more vicious attacks there.

226

African Spoonbill

Platalea alba

The European Spoonbill is a rare winter visitor to East Africa, sometimes venturing as far south as the lakes at Nakuru and Naivasha; whereas the African Spoonbill is a regular resident which nests on both those lakes as well as in many other resorts. The easiest distinguishing mark between the two species is the black beak and legs of the former compared with the lilac beak, bare red face, and red legs of the latter. The clownish quality in both their countenances is similar.

The bird illustrated here owned a nest with three eggs in the middle of Lake Naivasha. Other spoonbill nurseries in the same colony already contained two or three chicks—attractive, fluffy youngsters whose longish bills did not yet reveal any hint of the swollen, spoonlike tips-to-be. But some pairs of the species in the colony were still building their nests. I watched a couple on the job. The female stayed all the time on their wide, unfinished platform of sticks, sitting or standing as her moods changed. Her mate kept her company much of the time; but periodically he flew away, fetched a fresh long twig, and brought it back to her. Alighting at the nest edge, he offered it to her from the tip of his lengthy bill; and she accepted it in hers, and began to fit it into a suitable place in their home. That deed of partnership was repeated over and over again, the cock and hen birds observing exactly the same division of labour as is adopted, for example, by numerous types of doves.

Once they varied their occupation, and engaged in a little love-making. She was standing on the nest, and he jumped on to her back, and stood precariously upright there. They looked like a couple of circus acrobats uncertainly balanced prior to some daring double leap. But the trick which they then essayed is not on the programme of any circus. The hen stuck her comical-looking long beak straight out in front of her whilst the cock bent his head and seized it in his own slightly opened bill. At some moments he gripped her beak firmly between his mandibles, and at others he merely held a mandible close on either side of her closed beak, presumably ready to renew the grip if he felt that he was losing his balance. From that extraordinarily unstable position he lowered his hind-quarters, and attempted the act of mating. Whether he succeeded in his purpose was beyond my inexpert judgement to divine.

A spoonbill's food consists mostly of water insects, which it gathers in the shallows by wide sweeps of its beak from side to side as it wades purposefully forwards. No doubt its ample spoon gathers veritable banquets of its favourite tit-bits.

Yellow-necked Spurfowl

Pternistis leucoscepus

One of the earliest bird-calls greeting the dawn, and one of the last heralding the dusk every day in most of Kenya's nature reserves is the raucous cry of the Yellow-necked Spurfowl. It has a loud, rather guttural, frantic beauty which seems to proclaim the freedom of the wilds. This francolin grows to about the size of a domestic hen, and it is the commonest member of its family throughout Kenya and northern Tanzania. Small coveys of them stroll along every track, meander through every glade, and wander in and out of every woodland edge in open bush country. When startled by the arrival of a car they prefer to escape on foot rather than by their wings, and a party of them will skedaddle hopefully for considerable distances along a road ahead of the advancing vehicle, like long-distance runners being paced by a coach. Only if they begin to feel desperate do they suddenly leap into the air, skim a short way on outspread wings above long grass at the road-side, and plunge into semi-concealment in the undergrowth. Once landed there, they do not continue their retreat, but stand and watch the motor car with cool serenity tinged by slightly astonished curiosity. Few birds show more unshy confidence at all the strange apparitions of Nature.

They lay their three to half-a-dozen or more pale, hard-shelled eggs in scrapes on the ground lined with bits of grass, usually beneath the shelter of a bush. The newly hatched chicks are as lively and elusive players of hide-and-seek in their natural surroundings as ever wore well-camouflaged down. Except for the adult bird's conspicuous bright yellow throat—which is a patch of bare skin—its dress also has useful protective colouring. That is perhaps a contributory cause of its customary tranquil self-assurance. At dusk those throats appear like little candle-flames set on bushes or fallen tree-trunks wherever a party of the spurfowls perches to roost. The photograph of a rooster reproduced here was taken late one evening when darkness had already fallen.

Ground Squirrel
Xerus rutilus

In her attempts to persuade this squirrel to come and have its photograph taken in the precincts of the Uaso Nyiro game lodge, Chris threw bits of bread on the ground at the exact distance of her camera's focus. For some time the furry little animal watched her interestedly from semi-concealment among near-by bushes—but refused to be tempted. Then several starlings flew down and began to steal the crumbs. At once the squirrel emerged from its hiding place, scampered to the feeding ground, and drove the birds away, like a leopard shooing vultures from its kill. The animal probably was not particularly hungry, for it collected several scraps of the bread in its mouth—so many that its cheeks bulged hugely—and then ran away a little distance, and buried them in the earth at a spot which was evidently a private larder. Afterwards it returned to Chris's scattering of bread, and ate several pieces. When she passed that way again later in the morning she saw the squirrel digging bits of the buried treasure from its larder, and eagerly munching them.

On another occasion when she threw more bread for the squirrel in the same place it responded obligingly to that persuasion, ran to the area, stuffed its cheeks with the booty, and then scampered away and buried it in a different store-hole elsewhere underground.

Much of the time Ground Squirrels bury themselves also, for they live in subterranean warrens dug several feet deep beneath the earth's surface, where considerable colonies reside together with tunnelled passages communicating between their separate apartments. They ascend above ground chiefly for food, eating not only submerged products like roots, bulbs, seeds and grubs, but also upper earth crops such as grains and vegetable matter of various kinds. They are said to steal eggs and chicks from domestic poultry yards, too, when they get a chance to do so.

Their own young are born in their deep burrows, and are jealously guarded there.

Several other kinds of squirrels live in Kenya, such as the Giant Forest Squirrel and various types of Bush Squirrels. They spend most of their time not below ground, but high above it in trees.

Superb Starling

Spreo superbus

It would astonish students of Nature whose ornithological knowledge is confined to the birds of Europe, North America or, indeed, most other parts of the world to catch a glimpse of any one of numerous species of East African starlings. Those observers would not believe that a mere starling could be such a gorgeous creature. Watching the bird's approach, they would suppose that some new type of brilliant parrot, oriole, barbet or other famous beauty was flying into their view; but when the bird alighted on the ground its very ordinary figure, self-important strut, and vulgar manners would quickly communicate to their surprised intelligence that this could be none other than a starling.

The Superb Starling is only one of a number of gloriously plumaged cousins to be seen in Kenya. Typical others are the Red-wing Starling, Bronze-tail Starling, Purple Glossy Starling, Lesser Blue-eared Glossy Starling, Hildebrandt's Starling, and several additional varieties. Perhaps the most richly adorned of them all is the Golden-breasted Starling, with washes of metallic green, blue, purple and violet on various areas of its body, golden-yellow underparts, and an elongated, sharply graduated tail of dull old-gold touched up with blue and violet. All these species have scintillating beauty judged by any standard.

Both sexes of the Superb Starling wear the same dress displayed by the model on the opposite page. Their habits are similar to those of their more dully costumed relatives in other parts of the world, for they are gregarious, garrulous, mischievous, impertinent, prolific, and blessed with all the other extrovertish starlingish virtues and vices. In the presence of Man they are usually tame and fearless, running all round people's feet in crowded tourist camps at Amboseli, Mara, Uaso Nyiro and elsewhere to pick up scraps of food thrown to them, pecking at tit-bits held in a person's hands, and hopping on to tables to share the trippers' breakfasts, luncheons and teas.

Their courtship display is spectacular, the birds jumping about on the ground with outstretched necks and drooping wings to draw attention to their charms. Their nests, however, are unspectacular, consisting usually of untidily woven spheres of twigs and grasses lodged at random in low thorn trees or bushes. But in those cradles' feather-lined interiors four shining blue-green eggs give promise of the graceful creatures who in due course will emerge from them.

Black-winged Stilt

Himantopus himantopus

Black-winged Stilts are abundant winter visitors from Europe to East Africa which frequent in goodly numbers the water-edges of lakes along the Great Rift Valley. A certain limited number of the species are all-the-year-round, breeding residents there.

With less of a touch of fantastic elegance than the superficially similar Avocet, because the stilt's long thin bill is orthodoxly straight, whereas the other bird's is fabulously up-curving, it nevertheless has good-looking grace. That quality owes much to the tall, delicate, spindly legs which give the bird its distinctive name. Often these waders paddle together in small flocks. Not so restless as avocets, they sometimes pose motionless for long periods in engaging tableaux like the group at Lake Naivasha shown on the opposite page. That quartet evidently felt so serenely relaxed that all its members had tucked a leg cosily into their breasts as they balanced on one limb—a habit which the species shares with their neighbours, the Masai warriors. Comparatively unshy, stilts will often remain so poised even when a human intruder approaches quite close—although they keep a cautious eye on him. Then suddenly they take fright, lift themselves like miniature helicopters into the air, and fly around slowly with their lanky legs trailing behind them. When really alarmed, they utter a succession of little plaintive calls.

They feed on tadpoles, water beetles and aquatic insects (such as mosquito larvae) which swim on a pool's surface. Presumably the explanation of their straight beaks compared with the upcurved instruments of avocets is that their victims can be captured easily by simple downward jabs of their bills, instead of having to be scooped up by sideways sweeps.

In their nesting styles Black-winged Stilts are amphibious, sometimes constructing saucers of reeds, stalks and mud which float on the water, and at other times excavating shallow, roughly lined scrapes on dry ground. The nests are usually built in small colonies; and when the chicks hatch they have the appearance of a nursery school of young stilts.

Marabou Stork

Leptoptilos crumeniferus

This unprepossessing stork has more the habits of a vulture than of a stork. When a party of the birds congregates beside a lake they hunt stork-like by spearing frogs and fish; but more often they act vulture-like as scavengers dependent on filching carrion. Considerable flocks of Marabous often circle high in the sky, keeping a sharp look-out on the earth below; and when they catch sight of a corpse they descend at great speed. They gather with vultures near a lion's or other predator's kill, wait more or less patiently until the actual slayer has satisfied its hunger, and then join voraciously—though generally more quietly than the vultures—in demolishing what remains of the feast. Their bills are not made for tearing meat; so they swallow whole chunks of the stuff at one gulp.

In between whiles they stand around in quite large companies looking extremely solemn, but not always behaving with the dignity usually expected of such solemnity. They will quarrel and squabble, fighting over cast-off objects like rags, bits of broken rubber tubing, old skins and the like; for they seem ready to test almost anything as possible material for consumption. Their horse-play is often amusing to watch. And their catholicity of taste results in their having praiseworthy economic value as extremely effective scavengers. Among other things they are merciless slayers of locusts, which they regard as particular delicacies; and so they should be treated with the respect due to true benefactors of mankind. In some regions, however, they are unduly persecuted, because the soft feathers sprouting beneath the adults' tails have commercial value as 'marabou down', whilst the flesh of young birds is regarded as a luscious dish by certain people with tastes as dubious as those of the birds themselves.

Marabou Storks nest in colonies on tree-tops or cliff-faces, building stick platforms rather small in relation to their own impressive size. A full-grown bird stretches about five feet tall. Flocks of them often assemble in Nairobi's National Park, where all their entertaining habits can be easily studied.

As I have already written in an earlier essay, but for the murderous fondness which these storks demonstrate for newly hatched baby crocodiles, the crocodile population of East Africa would quickly reach intolerable proportions. The birds swallow those tiny reptiles by countless thousands as they break from their eggs. Yet I suppose that if—owing to some sudden gastronomic aberration—Marabous lost their taste for the youngsters, Nature would adjust the situation by arranging some alternative means to accomplish the deaths of multitudes of unwanted crocs.

Saddle-bill Stork

Ephippiorhynchus senegalensis

Unlike many other species of storks, the theatrically costumed Saddle-bill is a solitary, not a gregarious bird. Although it can be found in most parts of Africa, it is nowhere numerous, being scattered widely over swampy districts. Uncommon everywhere in East Africa, it is rare in Kenya except at Amboseli, where several pairs breed each year. There they loiter around marshes and pools singly, in couples, or at most in small family parties.

The bird hunts in the sedate manner of a heron, strutting leisurely through grass as it scans the ground for its prey, and making a swift, deadly stab with its beak whenever it sights a victim. I have watched one feeding for nearly two hours on end near a pond. Every now and then it took a rest, preening its feathers, indulging in a snooze, or just standing idly; but most of the time it stalked slowly and deliberately across a spacious area, keeping a hopeful look-out for tasty morsels. That morning it did not have much luck, catching at rare intervals such tit-bits as frogs and grasshoppers. The bird's taste is catholic, and it refuses nothing that is edible on its moist feeding grounds, such as fish, reptiles, small mammals, young birds, and similar fare in addition to grasshoppers and frogs.

The stork gazing at the reader from the opposite page is a female, because its eyes are dark brown, whereas those of the male are yellow. It demonstrates well why the species got its name. Most conspicuous among its various striking features is the long red bill ringed with a black band and surmounted by a bright yellow 'saddle' below which dangle two yellow stirrup-like objects. The bare patch of red skin high on its breast is typical of adults of both sexes; and expert ornithologists tell me that Heaven alone knows what its function may be. The bird's whole dramatic make-up is most impressive when you see it in real life standing some sixty-six inches tall.

Pairs build a typically stork-style nest of sticks in trees or reed-beds, and on its platform the hen lays one dull white egg. But too little is known about the habits and life-stories of this pleasing creature; and I hope that some bird-watching enthusiast will make a study of it in Amboseli or elsewhere. East Africa is still a rich, and often virgin, field for careful ornithological research into the ways of many interesting species.

White Stork

Ciconia ciconia

This is the decorative, rather fairy-tale stork well known in Europe for its habit of building nests not only in trees, but also on the roofs of houses, where it is alleged to keep itself busy—in between bouts of hatching its own chicks—by carrying new-born babies to their human mothers, probably delivering them Santa Claus-style down the chimneys.

In East Africa the species has hitherto been regarded as only a winter visitor; and it is true that large flocks of the birds arrive there in the European autumn, and depart again in the European spring. But a suspicion is growing that other members of the breed might adopt this corner of the world as their permanent home. Certainly some are becoming all-the-year-round residents elsewhere in Africa; and it is even thought that the proven diminution of the birds' numbers in Europe is due to their having discovered salubrious conditions for nesting south of the Sahara. A number of White Storks have already been recorded as breeding for several successive years in South Africa, whilst others are reported as doing so irregularly in Rhodesia. No similar intelligence has yet come from East Africa; but possibly it will appear later.

The birds' autumnal arrivals in various parts of Africa are in any case inclined to be erratic, depending on the whims of grasshoppers and locusts. Those insects form their main diet, and unless vast quantities of the food are present in a neighbourhood the storks cannot maintain themselves there. Quite large flocks of the birds can be seen plodding after their prey across grassy plains, cultivated fields, and semi-deserts alike; and they are so zealous that they will pursue swarms of locusts until the very last individual in those pestiferous mobs has been liquidated.

White Storks also often follow a plough as it unearths desirable morsels, in the manner of rooks and gulls in Britain. But their reputation as suspected midwives has not yet accompanied them from Europe to Africa.

Beautiful Sunbird

Nectarinia pulchella

More than sixty different species of sunbirds make their appearances in East Africa. Nature, the supreme artist, never revealed its genius for creating beauty more surely than when it fashioned them. The males of many species are brilliant, gorgeous gem-like creatures; and perhaps it seems odd that only one of them should be singled out for description as the 'Beautiful Sunbird'. Numerous others are even more beautiful than this particular individual. But anyone inclined to criticise that choice of title should understand the problems of nomenclature posed for the christeners of these various exquisitely fairylike little birds. The fact is that there were not enough appropriate adjectives to go round. Thus, just as this species is called the Beautiful, so others are named the Superb, the Splendid, the Shining, the Regal, the Amethyst, the Bronzy, the Golden-winged, the Scarlet-chested, the Violet-backed, the Purple-banded, the Blue-throated . . . and so on. Even the Mouse-coloured Sunbird is a rather magnificent being.

A male Beautiful Sunbird is a six-inch-long, glittering, metallic-green bird with a scarlet breast-patch bordered on either side by yellow. Its belly is black on the sub-species found east of the Great Rift Valley, and green on that occurring to the west of the valley. Both those cocks have finely elongated central tail feathers.

Hen sunbirds are much less decorative than their mates. A female Beautiful Sunbird is a modest ash-grey creature with a whitish eye-stripe and a yellowish-white, partially streaked breast. One such hen built the dangling, mango-shaped nest shown on the page opposite, on a bare stem of a dead plant on an island in Lake Baringo. Perhaps deliberately, she hung it within a few inches of another stalk on which she and her mate might perch when they brought food to their two chicks. From there they could lean across to present the youngsters with the small caterpillars and insects which they fetched every few minutes to appease their insatiable appetites.

Unfortunately the lovely cock bird never put in an appearance during the several hours of Chris's photography. Probably he was still frightened by the appearance of her hide only six feet from their nest; or perhaps he was just plain lazy. The chicks indoors were growing big by miniature sunbird standards, and their mother had a ceaseless task satisfying their demand for food, food, and more food. Every few minutes she brought them a fresh ration. In the picture opposite one of the hungry chicks is yelling for yet another bite during one of her brief absences.

Bronzy Sunbird

Nectarinia kilimensis

As I have mentioned already, more than sixty different species of sunbirds are found in East Africa. Fortunately some of them are quite common in Nairobi gardens, where the males look like hovering jewels as they suck nectar from flowers. Indeed, their elegant small figures, gaily darting movements, and brilliant gleaming colours are as lovely as anything could be.

I became familiar with several kinds of sunbirds during my many years in Asia. They, too, possessed the identical quality of exquisite beauty; yet they were all different species from every member of the related assortment in Kenya. Nevertheless, although the two sets of birds lived on different continents separated by several thousand miles of ocean, they shared exactly the same habits. It is not a matter simply of similar physical characteristics; their social and domestic customs are also the same. For example, among the African and Asian species alike, during the breeding season the hens build their nests without any help from the cocks, the hens again do all the incubation of the eggs unaided by their mates, and only when the chicks have hatched do the male birds suddenly recover a sense of their parental responsibilities, and join in the labour of bringing food to the youngsters.

Thus, I watched a pair of Bronzy Sunbirds in my garden last year. I first noticed them during the latter days of January keeping constant company together, like a betrothed couple. On February 9th I found their unfinished nest, a closely woven structure shaped like a hollow mango suspended below some foliage on a slim jacaranda bough stretching about fifteen feet above a flower-bed. Alike in build to the nests of numerous species of Asian sunbirds which I knew, it had not only the same general shape and texture, but also the same circular entrance near the top of one side, a similar thatched portico protruding above that entrance to protect it from rain, and an identical tassel of grass suspended beneath it.

The hen bird was hard at work completing the job. About every minute for hours on end she arrived with a new fragment of building material, wove it deftly into place on the structure, and then flew away to fetch another piece. The cock never lifted a feather to help her. But he was far from indifferent to her labours. Much of the time he sat on a branch above the nest, watching her constant comings and goings, and lending her moral support by his lordly presence. And every now and then after she had tucked a fresh beakful of cobwebs or other soft stuff into the nest (for she was engaged in upholstering its interior) she would flutter up to his perch, settle for a few seconds companionably beside him, and then speed away again to fetch more building materials. I had watched a very similar relationship between male and female sunbirds of various species in Malaya, Borneo and India.

Only once during several long sessions of observation through the next several days did

I see the cock abandon his passive role. It was at a time when the hen had stopped building for a while, and whilst she was refreshing herself with sips of honey as she flitted from lily to lily in the flower-bed below their nest. A second male sunbird approached her, and made a pass at her. Immediately her mate launched himself at the intruder, and chased him furiously out of sight.

Later the hen did all the incubating of their single egg, the cock never condescending to take a turn at that tedious task. Twice I saw him fly to the nest, alight on its entrance and peer inside, as if his curiosity had momentarily got the better of him, and made him go to inspect that odd, lifeless-looking oval object within. But he never hopped indoors to do even a few seconds shift of duty. Again, he was following the custom of all the sunbirds that I knew, in sharp contrast to the habits of many other species of birds.

The situation changes after a chick hatches. When I first arrived in Nairobi some competent ornithologists told me that the male Bronzy Sunbird neglects even the duty of helping to feed his chick; and I was intrigued by the suggestion, because it seemed to indicate a sorry aberration from proper sunbird behaviour. Then I discovered that my informants were wrong. I found that after their nestling hatches the male parent joins the female in the tireless task of bringing small caterpillars, spiders, flying-insects and other delicacies to feed it. If visual proof of that be needed, the photograph opposite of a cock perched at a nest just after feeding his youngster provides it. At that nest the male came nearly as frequently as the female to nourish their chick—which is saying a lot, for she returned every few minutes. The photograph on the previous page shows a hen bird on that job.

This year the same pair of Bronzy Sunbirds, presumably, built another nest on the very next twig to their last year's lodgement in a jacaranda tree in my garden. I watched them as carefully as my official duties would permit; and sure enough, the cock bird joined in the task of feeding their chick. But so far as I could see he only started doing that two or three days after it hatched. Before that I am inclined to think the hen did all the fetching of food. Perhaps that explains the earlier misconception by some observers.

This year I happened to have more leisure than last year to watch the pair of attractive birds; and I discovered that the hen built three successive nests between late February and early July, laid a solitary egg in each one of them, and successfully hatched the first two chicks, whilst the third egg proved to be addled. Presumably such industry is due to the fact that Bronzy Sunbirds do produce only one egg in each nest, and that therefore a series of nests is required from every pair each year if their species is to be safely preserved.

The portrait on the opposite page shows the gleaming iridescence on a cock bird's head and neck. The colour of that sheen varies according to the angle of the sun's rays; but usually it has a bronzy hue—which gives the species its name. The photograph here indicates the male's graceful figure, beginning at one end with his fine down-curving beak, and finishing at the other with two elongated central feathers extending three inches beyond the rest of his tail. He looks what he is, a veritable aristocrat.

Mosque Swallow

Hirundo senegalensis

This is a somewhat larger swallow than most members of the tribe, measuring about nine inches long. Its flight is more lethargic than that of its very swift smaller relatives, and is marked by an appearance of periodic hesitation in the air, caused by the fact that after each series of quick wing flutters the bird glides for a while on motionless, outstretched pinions before vibrating them again in another bout of flapping. The habit makes the Mosque Swallow sometimes look like a tiny hawk hunting its flying prey.

Another of the bird's idiosyncrasies is that it perches on trees much more often than most swallows do. It is a resident of parklands, wooded regions, and cultivated areas where large individual timbers grow, rather than of built-up areas of human settlement. So it rarely constructs its nest on a house wall, resorting instead to holes in trees like old cedars and baobabs. It reduces those cavities to a convenient size by the introduction of mud, which it imports in large quantities into the tree-trunk. When it does occasionally build a different type of nest on a cliff face, beneath a bridge, or against a house, the structure is a thick-walled, retort-shaped, wide-mouthed retreat which takes a long time to complete.

One such edifice appears to be intruding into the photograph on the opposite page, but in fact that nest on the house wall was an abandoned Striped Swallows' nest similar to the one pictured on the next page. The Mosque Swallow shown here was not leaving that cradle for chicks, but another one concealed beyond the crack between the wall and the ceiling just behind it. Through that space a pair of the birds had carried a lot of mud, and arranged its particles in a small circle lined with feathers on a bare flat plank. On the thin carpet of feathers the hen had laid three white eggs.

Striped Swallow

Hirundo abyssinica

An odd fact about this good-looking swallow is the almost unbelievably long time it takes to make its nest. That nest—as is partly shown in the picture opposite—is a retort-shaped object with a large bulbous chamber entered through a long narrow tunnel, all stuck on a wall beneath an overhanging eave. It is composed of many hundreds—about a thousand altogether, I believe—of little 'bricks' of mud painstakingly gathered in individual beakfuls by its builders. Both birds of a pair help in the construction. Whilst one is doing a turn of duty its mate sometimes perches as a spectator on a near-by roof, and contributes musical accompaniments to its partner's labour by singing the gay but far from melodious little song of a Striped Swallow. John Williams aptly describes that ditty as 'squeaky, metallic notes, not unlike a violin being tuned'.* Periodically the soloist utters 'also a brief warbling song'; but that lasts only a few moments before the instrument goes out of tune again.

Naturally each mud-brick must be wet when it is added to the nest structure, otherwise it would not adhere. So in the absence of a pool in the vicinity building operations can only proceed after a good shower of rain. Following such downpours I have often watched a Striped Swallow descend again and again in a quick succession of visits to the same garden path, gather a mouthful of damp earth in its beak, fly with this to an unfinished nest, and by careful trowelling with its bill lay new stones, one by one, well and truly. For many days between one rainstorm and the next the birds can do no construction. That perhaps partly explains why these swallows take so very long to complete a nest. Another reason may be that in any case a builder cannot at one time add more than a limited quantity of fresh wet earth to the structure without risking the new bit of wall collapsing through lack of firmness. Several days of drying may be required to allow the latest addition to settle tightly into place before bearing the weight of further layers of bricks.

Whatever the reason, the birds seem in no hurry to finish a nest, working in fits and starts at irregular intervals, building energetically for a few days, then going on strike for several weeks, then engaging in more days of hectic construction, then ceasing labour again, and so on. By such processes pairs of Striped Swallows who shared my occupation of Government House took three or four months to complete a nest; and one couple which started building early in January did not finish their home until mid-June.

Quite often their labours then turn out to be in vain, because thieving White-rumped Swifts arrive, commandeer the new structure, and proceed to lay their eggs in it. But sufficient numbers of young Striped Swallows get laid, hatched and reared to maintain their beautiful species.

* *A Field Guide to the Birds of East and Central Africa*, by John Williams.

Wire-tailed Swallow

Hirundo smithii

In many parts of Kenya Wire-tailed Swallows are almost like domestic pets, for they build semi-cup-shaped mud nests close beneath the ceilings of house verandahs, become almost indifferent to the comings and goings of the home's human residents, and live on quite familiar terms with them. They sit serenely incubating their eggs throughout gossipy tea-parties on the ground a few feet away; and when their chicks hatch they fly constantly to and fro fetching food for them, regardless of people moving about immediately below.

Nevertheless, they are careful about the safety of their offspring, and become at once alarmed at any unaccustomed activity in the vicinity. For instance, although the two owners of the nest in Larry Wateridge's verandah portrayed on the opposite page had for days shown little or no concern at routine busy events there, they were immediately perturbed when Chris set up her camera and flashlamps for photography. Nonplussed by the strange new apparatus, they sat cautiously watchful on a telephone wire several yards outside the verandah, and for a few hours they refused to go near their nestlings after Chris had disappeared into her hide. On occasions they showed not only concern, but also courage in defence of their young. For example, when I stood at what I considered a proper distance about thirty yards away in the garden, and held up my field-glasses to observe developments, one of the swallows took off from the telegraph wire, made circles of swift flight in the air above me, and every now and then dipped to within a few inches of my head, screaming loudly as it went by. Obviously it regarded me as an undesirable immigrant, and was trying to order me out.

By the second day, however, the birds became reconciled to the new apparitions surrounding their home, and resumed their normal activities. At first when they brought food for their youngsters, and when Chris's flashlamps thereupon filled the verandah with sudden lightning strokes, they took fright and stayed away for a while. But when the hen realised that those explosions did neither herself nor the chicks any harm, her maternal instinct reasserted itself, and she fluttered to the nest, perched on its edge, and tarried there feeding the nestlings, completely indifferent to how often the flashlamps blinked. Later the cock also summoned up courage to resume his share of the labour. So the swallows' lives returned to normal, and the photography also proceeded without further interruption.

Both adult birds were indefatigable in their parental duties. Every few minutes from dawn to dusk—except for a period of siesta in the middle of each day—they arrived one after the other with a fresh insect for the nourishment of their ever-hungry youngsters. The picture opposite shows the hen bird approaching the nest with a scrap of food gripped in her beak. Her outer tail feathers are short compared with the corresponding very long, wire-thin feathers on the cock bird which give the species its name.

Square-marked Toad

Bufo regularis

I am an ignoramus about the scientific classification, life-history, customary behaviour, and every other significant fact concerning the two gossips portrayed in the conversation piece on the opposite page; but I am informed that their English name is Square-marked Toad, and that the Latin title is *Bufo regularis*. Otherwise all I can relate is that they hid themselves all day long every day among stones and plants in a small garden surrounding the bandas where our party stayed at Amboseli, and that each evening they emerged to lead a remarkably active life within the area of light cast by electric lamps on the floors of our verandahs and rooms. Their sole interest appeared to be the flies and other insects which alighted and crawled on the ground around them. Hop by hop one would advance towards those innocent visitors, stalking them with cautious yet seemingly clumsy tread which often in fact betrayed its presence to the intended victims. However, the ignorant, unintelligent little mites who were doomed to be eaten merely skeddadled or flew a few feet away from the pursuer, and then halted again, assuming that they had reached safety. After a short hesitation to adjust its sight and tactics, the toad would resume its plodding advance—and as often as not in due course with a quick flick of its tongue it claimed a prize.

Sometimes half-a-dozen or more such toads were hunting in the same neighbourhood. Apparently entirely fearless of Man, they would jump through the doorways into our rooms, and engage in their sport all round our feet. Every now and then the paths of two of them would cross, and they would then halt for a while to exchange the sort of gossip engaging the pair in this picture. Soon afterwards they once more parted, and went their separate ways.

I am told that Square-marked Toads, like many similar members of their widespread family, protect themselves from would-be predators by emitting an irritating substance from their parotoid glands—the two oval swellings sited behind their eyes. Their youngsters do not at first possess that weapon, and suffer awful annihilations as a consequence. Adult toads breed during the rains, mating zealously, and spawning massive numbers of eggs. Later the newly hatched tadpoles are accosted by innumerable enemies in the forms of aquatic beetles, freshwater crabs, dragonfly larvae, and various water-birds—and it is a fortunate toad that survives to maturity, to produce in its own turn another crowd of mostly condemned progeny.

Topi

Damaliscus korrigum

These russet-coated, blue-black haunched, yellow-stockinged antelopes are found in certain limited regions in Kenya, and are fairly common in the Mara Reserve. Pure grazers, they are beasts of the grassy plains and open savannah, usually consorting in parties of about twenty, but sometimes massing in much larger herds. That is particularly the case in some areas of Uganda, where vast companies of topis are a splendid wild-life spectacle. Members of the genus called 'bastard hartebeests', they are similar in appearance to, though handsomer than, their hartebeest relatives. They are powerful, robust creatures, with a pretty turn of speed when they gallop. Indeed, they are among the swiftest moving of all antelopes. Easily alarmed, the sound of their thudding hooves as they beat a hasty retreat echoes like a formidable cavalry charge.

I have read that when startled, topis emit alarm calls. The question of the comparative noisinesses or silences of different species of antelopes is one of the minor aspects of animal behaviour which still requires a lot of careful observation and research. Mr. A. C. Brooks writes in his *A Study of the Thomson's Gazelle in Tanganyika* that 'only on the very rare occasions when the air was perfectly still was the writer able to detect any sounds coming from a Tommy. Often when he had surprised a herd of Impala he heard a herd bull emit a grunt and a snort as if to call the herd's attention to his presence. Similarly, when observing a group of Grant's Gazelle the writer had heard an animal sound the alarm with a barely audible grunt or bleat, which was followed by the herd cantering off. Other species which make alarm calls are Topi, Kongoni and Wildebeest, all of which emit nasal snorts that sound like a man blowing his nose vigorously. The Wildebeest may even emit a deep grunt. Dik-dik will sound an alarm by a low-pitched whistle. In the case of Tommy, however, the writer has never been able to detect clearly any such notes of alarm. Their alarm signal seems to be rather a quick movement or shake of the body accompanied by a flick of the side stripe.' He explains that this alarm-raising body-shake is made by the leading female in a harem, and that at such a signal the whole herd scampers away. No doubt it is usually given when foes like a cheetah, a pack of wild dogs, or some other deadly killer on the hunt appears within view.

So it would seem that in similar circumstances topis sound the tocsin by snorting in the manner of a vigorous human nose-blow.

Leopard Tortoise

Testudo pardalis

When her time comes to give birth a female Leopard Tortoise digs a circular hole about eight inches deep and six inches in diameter, and ejects into it anything between five and thirty eggs. They look like a heap of ping-pong balls with hard, brittle, china-like shells. After staying buried for nearly nine months the youngsters hatch; and they then laboriously burrow their way up to the earth's surface. There they meet numerous enemies in the forms of predators on the ground and eagles in the sky; but the species nevertheless manages to remain common in many parts of East Africa.

These tortoises nibble and swallow varieties of vegetable matter from grasses to succulents. They are also fond of chewing small, soft bones which they find lying around in large quantities as remnants from meals gorged by beasts and birds of prey. Those bones are no doubt eaten for the calcium they contain; and they contribute mightily to the tortoises' physical well-being. A private owner of pet tortoises found that when he fed a young one with small chicken bones its rate of growth more than doubled. And the ultimate result can be rather titanic. Male leopard tortoises have been known to weigh eighteen pounds, and some females have turned the scales at more than forty pounds. Whereas in the case of the species called *Homo sapiens* the fair sex is only occasionally also the heavy sex, among Leopard Tortoises that is the invariable rule.

A lusty specimen like the animal shown opposite is an awe-inspiring sight as it ambles through the wilds carrying its decorative as well as useful house on its back.

Vultures

One of the surest ways of learning the whereabouts of a lion, leopard or cheetah at its kill is by sighting an audience of vultures gazing down from tree-tops overhead. Almost certainly then one of those lordly hunters is enjoying a feast on the ground below.

Normally vultures are widely scattered in the four quarters of the heavens. Their eyesight is very keen, and from a distance one of the birds will observe a predator making a kill, or will notice some other carrion-eater like a raven or a kite moving purposefully towards such a quarry; and at once it flies to the spot. Settling on a tree, a bush or the ground in the immediate vicinity, it awaits the completion of the beast's meal in the expectation of enjoying afterwards a grand guzzle at the corpse's remnants. Meanwhile other vultures from every point of the compass have sighted this promise of good things to come, and have also hastened to the site. Before long a considerable company of the great scavengers is assembled; and additional carrion snatchers like jackals, hyenas and Marabou Storks hover around. When the killer's appetite is satisfied, and it withdraws from the scene, all the vultures and other attendants rush to tear at the remaining flesh, until nothing except bare bones is left.

The behaviour of vultures at a kill may appear obscene when judged by the standards expected of human guests at a dinner table; but that is of course a false standard of appraisal for vulture conduct. These birds perform to perfection the part allotted to them in Nature's scheme of things, and their activities are incidentally of immeasurable benefit to Man himself. They are the most thorough of all scavengers, and but for their efficient service multitudes of disease-spreading corpses would lie around fields, villages and towns unattended. The results could be as disastrous for the human race as an atom-bomb war.

Hooded Vulture
Necrosyrtes monachus

Seven different species of vultures occur in East Africa. The commonest of them is the Hooded Vulture, two of which are perched on the opposite page. It is both a particularly omnivorous and also a particularly dirty feeder. Flocks will swallow with gusto all sorts of cast-away refuse on village and town garbage dumps, quarrelling over the dirty stuff in a seemingly loathsome manner. Their readiness to dispose of such material makes them particularly beneficial to their human fellow-townsmen, and for that reason they should be carefully protected. Unlike some other vultures, they are also not averse to swallowing living creatures like lizards and minor reptiles.

Nubian or Lappet-faced Vulture
Torgos tracheliotus

The Lappet-faced Vulture is perhaps the least common member of the tribe in East Africa, where it is a resident, but a very local one. Much more abundant in the farther north and north-west of Africa, it sometimes resides in the old Northern Frontier District of Kenya. There it frequents big-game areas; and the photograph on the opposite page was taken in the Uaso Nyiro district beyond Isiolo.

The bird is usually seen singly, with the formidable mien portrayed here. The largest of East African vultures, it measures more than three feet long; and it also boasts the most massive beak of any scavenger. Owing to its uncongenial temper all other vultures prudently give way to it at a kill.

Ruppell's Griffon Vulture
Gyps ruppellii

If one is seeking superlatives among the different types of vultures, Ruppell's Griffon Vulture is the noisiest of all the gang when an assortment of the birds squabbles over a feast. Its harsh squawks transcend the squeals and hissings of other contributors to their discordant chorus. A relatively widespread species, its members resort to plains and mountains alike, although they avoid human habitations.

The group of adult and immature Ruppell's Griffon Vultures shown in the photograph on the next page were a small fraction of a mob attending the funeral rites of a dead zebra. Three- or fourscore birds, mostly Ruppell's Griffons, but including also two or three other kinds of vultures, composed the assembly, which had the character of a public meeting in which a violent difference of opinion had broken out, with bandyings of arguments, hurlings of insults, exchanges of fisticuffs, and a complete breakdown of law and order. That state of affairs was temporarily halted when Chris and Bill Langridge drove up in a land-rover to take photographs of the crowd. Momentarily the birds were startled by this intrusion, and they ceased their struggling and guzzling, to eye the newcomers suspiciously. When they felt reassured they returned with unabated zeal to their more customary conduct in the presence of a deceased zebra—and no doubt within a short time that portly, full-fleshed beast was reduced to a mere empty skeleton.

So long as a lion or other masterful hunter is busy at a kill most vultures await their turn at a respectful distance. Only after the rightful owner of the meat is satiated, and has disappeared to sleep off its over-indulgence, do they make a concerted assault on the remainder of the prey. Some individual vultures are bolder, however; or perhaps they are just more cheeky. Differences of character mark different individual birds and beasts of the same species, just as they do in the genus *Homo sapiens*. This or that vulture is venturesome or cautious, courageous or timid, prudent or rash, according to its inherited nature.

So occasionally a daring bird seeks to snatch a tit-bit from a kill whilst a lion, leopard or cheetah is still consuming the meat. None of those superior animals tolerates such interferences. They shoo the thief away with a smack of a paw—as is shown in a picture on page 185. Occasionally they even rise from their repast and chase away a queue of prospective diners.

I remember an occasion when a pride of lions were feeding on the carcass of a giraffe. The male lion had already eaten his fill, and lay snoozing a few yards away whilst two lionesses and some cubs took their turn at licking, tearing and swallowing hunks of the dead beast's flesh. Most of the corpse lay at their feet, and it contained more than enough food to fill their bellies to repletion. But it happened that one limb of the body had got separated from the rest, and lay fifty yards away, where a dozen Griffon Vultures were greedily assaulting it. Suddenly one of the lionesses looked up and noticed them. She ceased her feeding, and stared at them with astonishment, as if she could scarcely believe her eyes. She seemed to feel personally insulted. After a few moments hesitation she crouched, and then she started to crawl slowly on her paws and belly towards the birds, as if she were stalking an intended victim. Some of the vultures noticed her, and flew hurriedly up into near-by trees; but others were either so engrossed in their feeding, or else so bold, that they took no notice of her. The lioness continued her advance, halting briefly now and then to gaze intently at them, no doubt considering what would be the most effective way to discomfort them. Afterwards she resumed her stalk. Panic began to spread among more of the birds; and several of them spread their wings and made hasty departures. But still a few obstinate individuals lingered. At last the lioness arrived within ten yards of them, gathered her strength, and made a sudden rush at them, with a final half-earnest, half-playful pounce as the most tardy scavenger fluttered into the air just in time to avoid a swinging paw-blow. Having succeeded in dismissing them, the grand huntress at once turned on her heels, strolled back to the dead giraffe, and resumed her own meal.

She cannot have intended to do serious bodily harm to the birds, since she would probably regard their flesh as repugnant. But she resented their presumption in starting to enjoy a feast before she and her fellow lords and ladies of the wilds had completed theirs.

Hooded Vultures usually build large stick-platform nests lined with leaves, grasses and other such materials on high trees or rock faces. Often they do so in scattered colonies, in which only one pair occupies each tree. Lappet-faced Vultures construct similar nests, more often on the tops of thorn-trees, and in more dispersed solitude. In all those repositories a single egg is laid. Ruppell's Griffon Vultures repair in the breeding season to lofty inland gorges, where they furnish slight niches on rock faces with a few sticks and feathers to make a lodgement for one, or occasionally two, eggs. I have often observed a large colony of them perched on successive tiers of ledges up a skyscraper cliff at Hell's Gate, near Naivasha, where they are next-door neighbours to a pair of those most majestic birds of prey, Lammergeiers.

266

Warthog
Phacochoerus aethiopicus

Warthogs are some of the ugliest creatures in Africa; but like many human beings who can lay no claim to physical beauty they possess admirable qualities of character often lacking in individuals of sublime pulchritude. For one thing, they are good family animals—a father, mother and their three, four or more hoglets living together in devoted companionship. Again, they combine a pacific disposition with courageous pugnacity in the face of danger. Being strict vegetarians, they are enemies to none of their fellow-beings—not even to Man, since they do not normally destroy cultivated crops, preferring wild grasses, roots and fruits. On the other hand they have a formidable selection of foes, being chased by lions, leopards, cheetahs and hunting dogs. That makes them wary, with the result that they do not usually stand and gaze inquisitively at strange passers-by, as many beasts in Kenya's parks do. At the slightest suspicious appearance or gesture they utter a grunt of alarm, turn tail, and run away. In such retreats they trot quite fast with their tails stuck stiffly erect, so that when a family of warthogs disappears in long grass those tails protrude like periscopes on a flotilla of submarines cruising through the vegetation. Only their hairy tips flutter like small pennants.

Nevertheless, when the warty-faced little animals are attacked and wounded, they fight back with great valour. To their last squealing breath they will defy an enemy of greatly superior strength. And if the hog escapes, it takes refuge in an old aardvark's or hyena's disused burrow, swinging round as it arrives at the entrance and entering the hole backwards, facing the foe to the end. One of them has been known to run out again in double-quick time a few moments later when a porcupine happened to be in residence at its rear! Pairs of warthogs usually breed in dungeons of that sort; and they and their hoglets use them afterwards as dormitories for slumber at nights.

Their short, sharp lower tusks (rarely more than six inches long) are their principal weapons of defence. The much longer upper tusks are mainly tools for digging up the bulbous roots which are among their favourite foodstuffs. When thus delving, a warthog kneels on its forelegs as if in prayer, and it crawls on its knees along the ground as it ploughs up a veritable banquet of roots, in the attitude of a Buddhist pilgrim approaching a holy place.

When the little brute is unalarmed, and condescends to pose for its photograph, it stands unabashed, seeming to say with Cromwellian modesty, 'Picture me just as I am, warts and all'. So it was with the trio portrayed opposite.

Common Waterbuck

Kobus ellipsiprymnus

This robust, shaggy-coated antelope is perhaps most easily recognised from the rear, where a large oval white ring encircles its rump. As has often been irreverently remarked, it appears as if it had just risen from a lavatory seat covered with wet paint. There is another, somewhat similar beast called the Defassa Waterbuck, which sports wholly white buttocks in place of the white-ringed variety. The two species, or perhaps sub-species, sometimes associate together in Kenya's wilds; and indeed in the Nairobi National Park they have begun to inter-breed, with rather confusing results on their hind-quarters.

Both animals are gregarious, consorting usually in groups of between ten and thirty individuals, in which one mature bull lords it over a harem of cows with their calves. Temporarily disinclined or frustrated bulls travel round in 'stag' parties of about half-a-dozen, whilst old males past the age of mating often stay solitary.

Of a sociable disposition, herds of waterbucks frequently mix with parties of impalas, wildebeests and other similarly disposed creatures. Rather heavy drinkers, they are especially plentiful in river valleys and other lush regions, although they also wander into broken stony country—but never far from water. Being good swimmers, they often take refuge from foes like African Hunting Dogs by plunging into lakes, ponds or streams, and submerging most of their bodies in the depths. Bulls are sometimes preyed upon by lions, whilst leopards, cheetahs and wild dogs go for the cows and calves. But the alleged unpalatable taste of waterbuck flesh is said to give them some degree of protection against the sort of wholesale attacks which wildebeests, zebras and most other antelopes suffer.

Reichenow's Weaver

Othyphantes reichenowi

Weavers, sparrows, and their close relatives are the largest tribe of birds in East Africa, more than 160 different species having been recorded.

Several of them inhabit my garden in Nairobi. The commonest there is the Reichenow's Weaver. It is not only the most plentiful, but also the most confusing. A pair will build not one nest, but two, three, four, five or half-a-dozen in the same tree, one after the other at top speed in close proximity. For example, last year in a palm tree on my lawn a couple erected five nests over a period of eight weeks. The result looked like a small colony of residences of several pairs of weavers, but was in fact all the property of those two owners. The cock did most of the building of their thick-walled, globular-shaped, untidily finished edifices; but the hen usually attended him as he worked, and she also helped him now and then. Each bird used this or that nest in the group for roosting at nights, although they did not always sleep in the same two retreats. It was difficult, however, to discover which nest they proposed to adopt as a cradle for their eggs—and in the end they used none of them for that purpose! Their labour seemed to have no object except as a means of expending their tremendous energies. They just had a passion for building.

This year the same pair of birds, presumably, erected a group of six nests at about the same places in the very same tree—and again they used none of them as a nursery for a young family. Nevertheless many Reichenow's Weavers' nests are of course repositories for eggs and chicks. No special season seems to be allotted for their laying and hatching, since I have observed parents feeding fledgelings in January, in March, in June and in later months of the year. The photograph opposite shows a cock bird visiting his mate in their chick-laden nest one mid-June. Chris was at first averse to its reproduction in this book, because the tail of the male is cut in the picture, and because his wings are not spectacularly outspread—both features which offended her perfectionist taste in animal portraiture. She took several perfect snapshots of individual cocks or hens, and wished to use one of those; but the charm of the picture opposite showing a pair of birds in domesticity together made her friends prevail upon her to give it preference.

Other attractive species of weaver birds in my garden are Holub's Golden Weavers, and Spectacled Weavers. The former build groups of nests in some ways like those of the Reichenow's, although their structures are neater, and they dangle and wave lightly in a breeze at the tips of palm-stalks instead of being woven firmly among the fronds. Spectacled Weavers are less exuberant, constructing only one nest. Other weaver birds in Kenya are tumultuously sociable, breeding in very crowded colonies. The habits of the various species in the family differ widely, and too little is known about their comparative idiosyncrasies.

Spectacled Weaver

Hyphanturgus ocularis

The cock Spectacled Weaver shown in the picture here began to build its nest in my garden on March 10th last year. When I first caught sight of it after breakfast that morning only half-a-dozen strands of building material looped between two neighbouring segments of a palm-frond composed the frail embryo of a nest. I watched the bird at work. He gathered his material from another large frond in the same tree, flying to it, perching on its central stem, gripping the edge of a leaf-segment in his beak, and then by a skilful series of tugs tearing off an eight-inch-long, grass-thin strip of leaf. This he carried to the nest site. With his feet widely straddled as one gripped each of two separate sections of the frond supporting the nest-to-be, and balancing there like a circus acrobat with toes inserted into different rings on trapeze ropes, he poked one extremity of the new building material on to the stalk where he judged this latest addition could best be fixed, and with quick, energetic, expert jabs, pokes and tugs with his bill tied it there. Afterwards he interwove it with the already positioned bits and pieces of nest-fibre. Each individual operation took him quite a time—I reckoned an average of two or three minutes—and only when he was satisfied that the new loop would hold firm did he cease that bout of toil, jump off his perch, speed back to the other frond, and rip off another length of leaf.

Early that afternoon I saw the cock and hen both at the nest. At the moment she was working harder than he, poking, knotting and threading a strand of freshly gathered fibre into place with the same industrious cunning as her lord. Later he joined in the task; and by that evening the nest consisted of several strips of material hanging together in a long, loose coil tied to the central frond-stem and suspended between two separate leaf-segments sprouting from it.

Two evenings later the nest had become a complete elongated loop of strands dangling like a fine necklace of interwoven grasses. During the next twenty-four hours the narrow necklace was extended gradually on both sides into a wider collar, with its circle on one edge beginning to contract so that its surface curved inwards, assuming slowly but steadily the shape of a large grassy egg open on each flank. By the next day's end the woven egg-shell was complete except for a gaping hole on one side only; and twenty-four hours later that hole had been partly covered by a jutting porch which was to be the topmost portion of a long downward-pointing funnel which forms the entrance to a Spectacled Weaver's nest.

Both birds worked like beavers at the construction throughout many more days, the hen being particularly active when the time came for upholstering the nest's interior. I am not sure how long they took to complete this cradle for their chicks, since during the last several days all their work was concerned with its internal strengthening and lining; and so they toiled indoors, invisible. But I saw the cock taking grassy stuffs into it eighteen

274

days after the first commencement of their building. By then the hen had, I believe, roosted in it every night for eleven nights.

Breezes must have blown the structure unduly this way and that, causing the birds apprehension about its security, for a few days later the cock brought more building material to anchor its lower parts to a neighbouring palm-frond, once more using astonishingly professional techniques in the construction. The hen had already laid her two eggs; but since these were hidden within, I could not tell precisely when they hatched. I first noticed the parents definitely carrying food for their twin chicks indoors on April 12th; but I think this new activity may have started a day or two earlier.

Both adult weavers shared the work of keeping their youngsters supplied, one or the other visiting them approximately every five minutes throughout the long feeding hours. A strange circumstance revealed an interesting difference between the respective natures of at any rate those two Spectacled Weavers compared with most other species of birds I know: the hen was at first distinctly more nervous than the cock about visiting the nest when Chris started exploding her flashlamps to take photographs.

The illustrations here show both birds bringing food to the nestlings. In the first picture the male has perched at the bottom of the entrance spout leading upward into the nest, before entering. The length of that spout varies on different nests made by different pairs of Spectacled Weavers. In this case it is unusually short, extending only an inch or two below the level of the bottom of the oval nest chamber. Sometimes the entrance stretches down a foot or more farther, like a long retort-funnel below the rest of the structure. This year in my garden a pair of Spectacled Weavers built a nest on the next palm-frond in that same tree, with an entrance pipe four inches longer than the one shown here. Presumably the birds were the same couple in each case. A possible explanation of the difference in their products is that the earlier effort was their first attempt at nest-making, that it was therefore rather non-proficient, that by experience and maturer instinct they were more professional in their building twelve months later, and that their second attempt had consequently lost the initial amateurish touch.

The illustration on the opposite page shows the hen bird flying up to last year's nest. In both years the parents reared their youngsters successfully, and about a fortnight after hatching the fledgelings flew gaily from home.

White-bearded Wildebeest or Gnu

Connochaetes taurinus

Though the wildebeest is popularly supposed to belong to the ox group, it is in fact a member of the variegated tribe of antelopes. The misconception arises from its appearance, which is rather confusing as well as somewhat grotesque. The animal's body is antelopian (in the style of its relative, the hartebeest), its long black mane and tail are distinctly horsy, its horns are cattle-like, and its face could be a mixture composed from diverse breeds. Indeed, its prominent whiskers and shaggy beard below a strong-nosed face make some African tribes associate it with another distinguished type of being, for they give it the nickname 'Talah Singh', identifying it with the Sikh community. In the Kenya species the beard has a very pale yellowish tinge, and its official title is the White-bearded Wildebeest.

Wherever these wildebeests, or gnus, occur they are plentiful, gregarious and sociable, mixing freely with zebras, hartebeests, topis, gazelles and ostriches. Existing themselves in perhaps larger numbers than any other species of animals, they engage in massive migrations at dry seasons when they need to search for adequate well-watered pastures. On the Serengeti plains more than a hundred thousand wildebeests have been seen wending their way in a packed procession covering several square miles from arid to better irrigated areas. They are said to travel some 200 miles on those annual treks.

Partly, no doubt, to keep them in training for these long journeys, wildebeests are frisky creatures. Periodically a herd will appear to indulge in a playful game of 'follow my leader', careering round and round in a limited space with an air of jolly abandon, tossing their heads, plunging their bodies, and flicking their tails. Considerable slaughter of the animals has taken place on account of those tails, because their thick, long hairiness makes them popular as fly-whisks with Africans, and now also with tourist trophy-hunters. Wildebeests are inquisitive. They will stand and stare for quite a while with dumb curiosity at a strange passer-by, then shy away and gallop a short distance with typical frolicsome gait, only to stop, turn about, and stare enquiringly once more. But they are not fools. In many parts of Kenya they share with zebras the doubtful honour of being a favourite food of lions; and they are far from accepting that distinction without vigorous contest. Many reliable reports by eye-witnesses tell of a bull wildebeest emerging victorious from a duel with a young lion, and driving the so-called king of beasts with contumely from the battlefield.

Dr. Louis Leakey writes that fossil remains show that the wildebeest 'has changed very little, if at all, in the past million years', and that it 'is in fact a "living fossil"'.*

* *Animals in Africa*, by Ylla and L. S. B. Leakey.

Grey Woodpecker

Mesopicos goertae

Twenty species of woodpeckers reside in East Africa. The Grey Woodpecker is a typical representative of the family, betraying its presence in copses by loud tappings on tree-trunks as it batters the bark in search of food.

The nest being visited by the hen bird opposite was tunnelled into a tall, broken tree. The installation of a camera and flashlamps in Chris's hide—which had been erected a day earlier to let the birds grow accustomed to it—alarmed the woodpeckers; and for half-an-hour after Chris settled inside her tent the silent stillness in the nest was as intense as that within the hide itself. Watching from thirty yards away, I wondered whether the nestling which had been seen on the previous day could have flown that morning, leaving its nursery empty. Then through my field-glasses I saw a cautious movement inside the shadowy nest-shaft; and a minute later a youngster very shyly popped its head through the entrance, and gazed carefully around. But not for another ten minutes did a parent bird venture to bring food.

After that an elder came regularly with fresh insects at about seventeen-minute intervals throughout the morning. None of the birds showed any fright at the flarings of the flash-lamps as Chris took picture after picture. Later, however, the lamp battery began to work ineffectively, and much talk developed between Chris in the hide and Bill Langridge on the ground below as they discussed ways and means of remedying the trouble. At that the nestling became concerned, and sought to escape from its confinement in the tree-trunk. The nest was situated two feet below the trunk's sawn-off top; and evidently a crack led through the rotting wood to that flat summit, for suddenly the youngster emerged on to the platform there. Its two parents at once alighted in neighbouring trees, fussing noisily. Then the hen went and fed her offspring on its stump top.

The enterprising young woodpecker sought further adventure. Raising its wings, it attempted flight—and promptly tumbled to the ground twenty feet below. I picked it up, climbed a ladder, and reinstated it in the nest. It seemed pleased to be home again; but as soon as Chris and Bill renewed their argument it once more took fright—and the whole episode was repeated move by move, ending up with my restoring the youngster once more to its nest. Its taste for freedom, however, was now whetted, and it immediately climbed again on to the exposed tree-top, where it sat stolidly. Both parents came periodically to feed it there.

Eventually Chris's flash equipment ceased functioning altogether, and she abandoned photography. I returned the young woodpecker to its nest, the family resumed their normal customs—and I trust they continued to do so until the fledgeling flew successfully a day or two later.

Zebras

Burchell's Zebra
Equus burchellii

No more charmingly picturesque animal exists anywhere than the zebra. It is Africa's version of the wild horse. Its pattern of black and white stripes is simple, yet also exotic; and if one did not see the actual beast walking around in the flesh, one would scarcely dare to conceive such a bold creation. It looks rather like an animal especially decorated for some spectacular circus turn. One of its charms is that it is not a rarity occurring only in pairs or small groups. Resident in many parts of East Africa, it is usually counted in herds of anything from half-a-dozen to a score of animals; and at certain times of the year not only hundreds, but thousands and even tens of thousands of zebras move *en masse* together.

Those grandest assemblies are formed only by Burchell's Zebras, the type which alone exists in southern and central Kenya, as well as throughout the more southerly parts of Africa. For a few weeks between the dry and the rainy season, when these zebras (like wildebeests) migrate in search of adequate supplies of succulent pasture, they trek in vast throngs from uncongenial, unwatered regions to areas where they know by instinct (or by whatever signs and portents guide zebras) that they will be able to satisfy both their hunger and their thirst. I have seen such a migration in progress in the Mara Reserve, where from dawn until dusk on two successive days I watched a non-stop column of the vividly striped creatures stroll past a spot where I sat observing a certain bird's nest. They walked sometimes two or three abreast, but more often in single file, almost touching each other head to tail, and processing at a steady, purposeful pace, like an endless march of political demonstrators.

A mother and foal of this species—Burchell's Zebras—are shown on the opposite page.

You never see a skinny, or even a slim zebra. Always the animals are plump, with well-developed barrel-shaped bellies, and fat hind-quarters. That is due to some particular capacity in their make-up to store fat content, perhaps in order to aid their survival during their long migrations. As a result zebras always seem to be bursting with rude health. And as another result, they are popular victims with lions. But they are well equipped with defensive weapons in the form of acute senses of sight, smell and hearing; and they react instantaneously to any hint of an enemy's approach, careering away at a quick gallop. That often saves them; but sometimes it only leads them into an ambush set by those very lions, as I have described earlier in this book.

Grévy's Zebra
Equus grevyi

Grévy's Zebra lives only in the north of Kenya, and in the neighbouring lands of Ethiopia and Somalia. In some regions there it shares the amenities of the wilds with its relative, Burchell's Zebra.

Various differences exist between the two species, the principal obvious ones being that Grévy's Zebra is considerably larger in size than the other beast, standing 14 hands as compared with 12 hands high at its shoulders; that its black, or dark brown, and white stripes are much narrower and more closely set than those on its cousin's body; and that its ears are large and rounded instead of being narrow and pointed. Another distinction is that although its stripes continue all the way down its legs and tail, like those on its relation, they do not extend to its under-belly, which is clear white. The photographs on the opposite page display the difference in appearance between the two types. The top picture shows a group of Burchell's Zebras drinking at a pool in Nairobi's National Park, whilst the lower one portrays a party of old and young Grévy's animals posing inquisitively at Maralal.

The voice of Grévy's Zebra also differs from that of Burchell's Zebra, for it brays rather like a donkey, whereas the other barks like a dog. Both species associate in similar parties, normally numbering between half-a-dozen and thirty beasts; but Grévy's Zebra does not engage in the same massive seasonal migrations, because it is not so dependent on water. That is why it is often found in much more arid zones than the lush, grassy plains and savannah favoured by Burchell's Zebras. It is also less skittish and more gentle in demeanour than its lively relation—but it shares with the other beast the awful distinction of being a popular meal with lions.

Comparatively little is known about the compositions and customs of zebra herds. Probably their habit of consorting in parties is a device for mutual protection, as is their gregarious readiness to mix with considerable groups of wildebeests and other antelopes. In the breeding season stallions who prove themselves superior to rivals in frequent little skirmishes dominate harems of obedient mares, with the usual fruitful results.

Grévy's Zebras are the most northerly type of zebras to be found anywhere in Africa, at least since the once green Sahara dried up ages ago and became a desert. The most southerly species of zebras used to be the quaggas of South Africa; but they, alas, were exterminated by merciless mass killings as men's agricultural settlements spread steadily farther northwards from the Cape of Good Hope during the nineteenth century. The last living sample of a quagga died in the Berlin Zoo in 1875, and now the handsome beast is extinct.

That is a sorry warning of what can happen when men become careless about preserving the Earth's treasure of wild life.